THE SPIRITUAL WISDOM OF
MARCUS AURELIUS
THE DIVINE CONVERSATION

Alan Jacobs

BOOKS

Winchester, UK
New York, USA

THE SPIRITUAL WISDOM OF

MARCUS AURELIUS

A POETIC TRANSCREATION

Copyright © 2004 O Books
46A West Street, Alresford, Hants SO24 9AU, U.K.
Tel: +44 (0) 1962 736880 Fax: +44 (0) 1962 736881
E-mail: office@johnhunt-publishing.com
www.johnhunt-publishing.com
www.0-books.net

U.S. office:
240 West 35th Street, Suite 500
New York, NY 10001
E-mail: obooks@aol.com

Text: © 2004 Alan Jacobs
Design: Graham Whiteman

ISBN 1 903816 74 2

A CIP catalogue record for this book is available from the British
Library.

Printed in Singapore by Tien Wah Press (Pte) Ltd

ABOUT THE AUTHOR

Alan Jacobs is a retired art dealer. He is now the Chair of the Ramana Maharshi Foundation UK.

He is editor and compiler of *Poetry for the Spirit*, Watkins Publishing, 2001, formerly *The Element Book of Mystical Verse*, Element Books, 1997; *Reflections: An Anthology of Contemporary Mystical Verse*, Rowan Press, 2000 and *From the Infinite Centre the Prose and Poetry of Thomas Traherne*.

His poetry is published regularly in the magazines *Reflection* and *Self Enquiry* and a collection *The Pearl Fishers*, published by the Broadfield Press, 1997.

His search commenced in 1957 and since then he has made an extensive enquiry into the teachings of George Gurdjieff, Jiddu Krishnamurti, Jean Klein, Ramana Maharshi, Douglas Harding, Arthur Schopenhauer, and Ramesh Balsekar.

He is a practicing "Life Coach" (The Life Coaching Academy) and a Neuro Linguistic Programming practitioner (McKenna Breen trained).

*Dedicated
to my wife Jane
who admires and enjoys
the writings of
Marcus Aurelius*

ACKNOWLEDGEMENTS

To Michael Mann for suggesting the book, to Eve Dennehy who has painstakingly typed the manuscript, to my teachers at the Life Coaching Academy whose ideas often coincide forcibly with those of Marcus Aurelius, and to the British Library for its extensive research resources.

CONTENTS

INTRODUCTION

Marcus Aurelius Antoninus was born in Rome in ad 121 and died in March 180.

His father was a Praetor (one of two magistrates in the City). His mother was Domitia Calvilla known as Lucilla. The Emperor Antoninus Pius married Annia Galeria Faustina, the sister of Annius Verus, and was thus Marcus Antoninus's uncle. When the Emperor Hadrian adopted Antonius Pius as his heir, Antonius Pius adopted as his successors an adopted son Commodius and our Marcus.

He was very carefully educated by private tutors, and when Hadrian died in ad 138, he married the cousin of Pius. He was then called Caesar and assisted in the administration of state affairs. His father died in 161. The Senate wished for Marcus to become the Emperor, but he joined with Commodius – the other heir – so Rome had two Emperors for the first time. Commodius was indolent and a man seduced by pleasure, but they remained as colleagues in peace. Marcus's daughter Lucilla later became the wife of Commodius.

Marcus's reign was troubled by the Parthian War, which ended in 165. Barbarians tried to invade Italy from the North and he was engaged in driving them back. Commodius died in 169 and Marcus then became the sole Emperor.

He was forced to fight wars in Asia, because of invasions. His wife Faustina died suddenly at Mount Taurus much to his grief. He progressed his journeys into Syria, Egypt, and Greece where he was initiated into the Eleusinian Mysteries. He re-entered Rome in triumph with the son of Commodius in ad 176. He defeated Germanic invaders in ad 179 but was infected by a contagious virus and died at his camp in 180, at the age of 59. His ashes were carried to Rome and he received the honor of deification.

He was revered as a hero by the Romans and many statues were erected in his memory. For further biographical information I suggest one reads the introduction by George Long (1862) in his authoritative translation of his *Meditations* along with an essay on his philosophy. Matthew Arnold, arguably the greatest essayist in the English language, also wrote a long essay on the importance of Marcus Aurelius.[1] Arnold was influential as the Inspector of Schools in the Victorian age in setting out the basic principles of English education. He laid the foundations of the English educational system, which was designed to produce administrators for the great British Empire. Marcus Aurelius was a Stoic. Briefly, Stoicism is an early Greek philosophical system founded by Zeno (c. 300 bc). It sees the Universe as permeated by reason and divinely ordered. Morality and happiness are achieved by living that rationality for oneself. Marcus Aurelius was obviously a major influence. English Stoicism, inherent in our educational system, particularly the public schools, may stem from Aurelius's influence.

I have approached this book from the point of view of removing the heavy dust on its covers. The three major translations I have studied, those of Loeb Classical Series, Long, and Staniforth are by Greek scholars and lack the emotional warmth to convey the essential meaning to our generation. Marcus mainly refers to "he," omitting "she"; in many verses I have reinstated the feminine gender.

---

[1] I have appended this brilliant essay as an appendix. It is the best appreciation of Marcus in the English language. It was written after the George Long translation was published. I have based my Transcreation on Long (Collins Library of Classics) but have consulted all other translations into English.

I have therefore "transcreated" it using the medium of contemporary free verse – swift line breaks and many added metaphors to convey the essential emotional meaning of the text. Most scholarly academic translations are literal and arid, encased in archaic language. This is a paraphrased selection of the best of his meditations so as to give more force to the essential truths of his philosophy. Certain verses are omitted where they are repetitive. The numbers remain unchanged so the reader may note verses left out. In some cases the verses are considerably abbreviated. In effect this transcreation is a distillation of the text in everyday language. Marcus used repetition to hammer his points home, so some repetition is unavoidable. I have enhanced the meaning for my contemporaries by adding my own understanding where appropriate and in harmony with the text.

Marcus Aurelius is highly appropriate to our troubled times. Recent events have highlighted the need for radical new values to counter the angst, stress, and depression of our age, which includes modern warfare against terrorism and a weakening economy. The Stoicism of Marcus is the best defense against gloom and doom, as well as reaffirming our true civilized standards. His meditations have remained in print for two thousand years inspiring many men and women of all cultures, classes, and nations.[2] He touches the frontier where reason and mysticism meet, as did Plato and Plotinus before him.

The footnotes are few and brief mainly to unravel historic points. In some cases the verses have been slightly modified according to my own understanding so as to make them more pertinent to our generation.

All translators of this great sage have subjectively re-interpreted him according to the cast of mind of their generation. I hope this effort will speak to my generation meaningfully, to draw moral

---

[2] An interesting article appeared in the Weekend Telegraph of 8 December 2001, by Cassandra Jardine, where she tells the story of the writer Jeremy Scott who was saved from suicide by reading the works of Marcus Aurelius after an excessive, hedonistic life which nearly ended in disaster.

inspiration during the hard challenges of the twenty-first century. This is essentially a book of maxims by a Stoic philosopher-emperor-sage. It is an ethical work based on the power of reason to limit the irrational power of willfulness. It is therefore a grand guide for those who wish to lead a happy and spiritual life, in tune with the higher ethical standards of our humanity. In short, Marcus's advice to men and women is to make a profound moral choice based on reason and then be firmly on the side of the good, come what may.

What Marcus is essentially pointing out is that the rational mind, ethical in its character, must triumph over the passions with full force. One only has to think of great minds who have been destroyed by failing to live up to the Stoic principles. Oscar Wilde is perhaps the best example.

I suggest reading a few verses a day. This is a wonderful antidote to the stress of contemporary life. After all, what is stress? Only the difference between one's true Self and one's false Self. Marcus Aurelius points this out forcibly, by implication, on many occasions.

As an accredited Life Coach[3] and NLP Practitioner[4] I find great positive and realistic thinking in his ideas.

I find the value of Marcus's Meditations is to strengthen our moral sense based on rationality, which is always challenged by unruly passionate emotions. Although man is driven by necessity he can reinforce his rational sense to make ethical decisions that benefit society and help him lead a happier life. Marcus sees the Universe as essentially holistic, governed by Nature and her laws. There is an inner freedom gained by the wholehearted acceptance of whatever happens even if we do not always approve. He recognizes a soul, which has an after existence; but this transmigration is a mystery. He stresses positive rational thinking based on experience. He is a useful antidote to the

---

[3] The Life Coaching Academy.
[4] McKenna Breen Neuro Linguistic Programming Training.

excess of confusing and destructive "hedonism" of our contemporary culture. He is fascinating to read because he shows us the cast of mind of an ancient Roman – an Emperor indeed, and a practicing Stoic.[5]

---

[5] As a second appendix I reprint the excellent note on Stoicism included in an early translation of the *Meditations* by the Harvard University Press (1916), C. R. Haines translation.

Marcus Aurelius

INVOCATION

A HYMN
Highest munificent God above
Lord of all manifest names, eternal, immutable in
    your glory.
You are the auspicious One.
Arch-creator and Source of our Universe,
Ordering the "whole" according to your laws.
To call upon you is beneficial for men and women for
    we all come
from you alone.

All sentient beings that dwell on Earth are given speech
to sing your praises and to marvel at your everlasting
power and splendor.[6]

[6] This hymn is attributed to Ceanthes, the disciple of Zeno, founder of the Stoicism which
Marcus Aurelius followed.

THE MEDITATIONS OF
THE EMPEROR
MARCUS AURELIUS
ANTONINUS ADDRESSED
PRIMARILY TO HIMSELF

BOOK 1. MY TEACHERS

1. It was dear Catilus Severus,
   my beloved grandfather,
   my mother's father,
   who first taught me
   always to be polite
   in relationships
   and even in the face of all events,
   good or bad as they may seem,
   to behave with equanimity,
   never to over-react, but
   deal with each happening, welcoming all
   appropriately as it comes.

2. From my adored father praetor, Annius Verus[7]
   I learned manly virtues
   without ever fanning my feathers
   like a peacock.
   In my dear sweet mother,
   Domitia Calvilla, called Lucilla,
   I saw a living example
   of devoted service and
   wholehearted generosity,
   She was never mean in thought or deed,

[7] One of Ancient Rome's two magistrates.

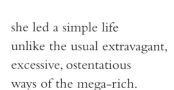

she led a simple life
unlike the usual extravagant,
excessive, ostentatious
ways of the mega-rich.

4. From my respected great grandfather
I received the good advice
to say "No" to a public school education,
and to be well taught at home.
No expense for employing the best tutors
should ever be spared.

5. It was my gifted teacher
who convinced me never to
be carried away
by either betting on the green chariot
or the blue chariot at the races.
Or over "the lightweights" or
"the heavyweights" at the
gladiatorial games.
And never to be work-shy,
but to be modest in my
daily needs.
Always to mind my own business
and never waste time or energy
in trivial tittle-tattle,
and witless gossip.

6. Thanks to the philosopher-artist Diognetus
   I learned to give up petty trifles
   and not to believe hearsay
   about wonder-workers, magicians,
   spells, exorcism of demons,
   charismatic teachers;
   never ever to breed fighting cocks
   for sport or enjoy such horrors
   as giving them steel spurs.
   To love freedom of speech,
   above all philosophy,
   especially that of Bacchius,
   Tandasis, and dear Marcian.[8]
   To practice essay-writing
   while still young
   and to sleep on hard wooden planks .
   covered in goat skin,
   enjoying other rigors of our noble Greek discipline.

7. From Junius Rusticus
   the Stoic, and my law tutor
   I learned that "character"
   needed to be built carefully,
   and not to be misled by
   false reasoning or idle speculation,

[8] Contemporary Roman philosophers whom Marcus often visited.

BOOK I. MY TEACHERS

nor to revel in making
moral judgments,
nor vainly show off to
ascetics or do-gooders;
to avoid tub-thumping,
doggerel verse, and purple prose.
Instead to copy the fine
writing style of Junius's
wonderful letter to my
mother when she was at Sinuessa.
He taught me not to flout
about at home
in outdoor clothes
but to change into relaxed robes.
With anyone who has offended
me verbally
or did me a bad turn
I should speedily, peaceably
forgive them and be reconciled,
once they seem ready to accept.
I should read, carefully,
with full attention,
and not be satisfied by
superficial skimming.
I should not quickly agree with
those who talk too much
just to keep them quiet.

Junius also helped me by
giving me the works of the great Epictetus
which he lent me from his own library.[9]

8. From Apollonius another Sage
I learned about the metaphysical mysteries
concerning the Will
and its possibility of freedom.
I learned about steadiness of
aim and to rely on my reasoning
powers,
and to be equal in severe pain,
whether in the loss of a loved child,
in grave illness,
or in ecstatic joy;
and to see clearly that one and
the same man
may at different times be
both strong and then yielding;
And never to be embarrassed by
giving orders.
I am grateful to have experienced before
my very own eyes a man
who lived from his own experience

[9] Epictetus (c ad 50–120), one of the Stoic philosophers. They developed their ideas of
personal responsibility and inner freedom based on morality. He emphasized the need to be
free from the passions and gain equaniminy in the face of inscrutable destiny.

BOOK I. MY TEACHERS

and had the skill to tell it to
others simply and modestly.
I also learned
how to greet friends and
accept their goodwill
without mock humility
or disregarding their obvious affection.

9. From Sextus of Chaeronea
    grandson of the famed historian Plutarch[10]
    a man of good humor
    and kindness,
    from a noble family,
    living in harmony with Nature,
    serious without affectation,
    guarding his friend's rights,
    tolerant of the illiterate,
    and even those who spout thoughtless opinions,
    like burbling fountains.
    He mixed well with all,
    friendship to him was better than
    flattery.
    He was highly respected,
    he could reveal, order
    intelligently, and systematically state

10 Marcus's good fortune was to meet the most talented intelligences of ancient Rome.

the principals and fundamentals
of life.
He was never angry
nor ever passionate
and genuinely affectionate.
He could say thank you, graciously;
he was wise
without showing off his knowledge
like a braying ass.

From Alexander, celebrated grammarian
a critic of great Homer, no less,
I learned to shun
fault-finding with my fellows,
and not to scold,
but to gently chide those who overstated
their case.
He enjoyed discussion,
he enquired directly into the
"Thing in Itself," not merely talking about ideas
or second-hand speculative suggestions.

From Fronto,
a fine orator and friend
I learned to see
that envy,
double dealing,

BOOK 1. MY TEACHERS

hypocrisy,
are the tyrants in a tyrant,
the terrorists in terrorists,
and those who call themselves Fathers
Often lack paternal love.

12. From Alexander,
a pupil of renowned Plato,
I learned never to say,
"May the Gods forbid"
or write in a letter
that I am much too busy
and have no time for you.
I also learned never
to neglect my duties
to my relations and those
with whom I live,
by pretending I have
more important things to do.

From the Stoic Catulus
I learned not to be upset
by friends
who complain and nit-pick,
but instead I try to help
them find a better place in
themselves.

Also I learned always
to speak well of my
teachers
and to love my own children
wholeheartedly.

From my friend and brother in
the Self, Severus,
I learned
to love my kinsfolk,
Truth, and Justice.
He led me to firm friends,
the noble Thracea, Helvidius,
Cato, Dion, and Brutus[11]
from them I learned how to rule,
and the principle of Justice,
that there is one law for all,
with care for equal rights.
and freedom of expression
come what may.
He also taught me the ways
of Kingship
which respects the freedom of his subjects.
I learned from him to love Philosophy.
The will to do good and help others

[11] The lives of Marcus's noble friends may be found in Plutarch and Tacitus, the historians of ancient Rome.

BOOK I. MY TEACHERS

in this painful pilgrimage to Truth.
He also said "be optimistic,
affirm life as it comes to you,
be chock a block full of hope
and remember that your friends all love you."
But to those of whom he
disapproved
he was plain, simple, and
forthright.
He was used to virtuous deeds,
forgiving,
free of lying,
and firm like a large rock
in a rough sea.
He could never be diverted
from what he knew to be right,
he was not just a man who had merely
been improved" by others.
He never hated anyone
or thought himself to be superior.
He was ego-less
and humorous,
to be all things to all men at all times.
He loathed fault-finding with his fellows
and never scolded.

15. From the esteemed Claudius Maximus,
my brother Stoic,
as close to an ideal man
as I have ever met,
I learned not to be obstructed
by anybody
from the course of action
I knew to be right.
To be glad in all happenings,
so called good or bad,
and in sickness.
To mix, wisely, the qualities
of sweetness and dignity,
and never to complain
about "what is."
I learned from him that everyone believed
they never had wicked intentions
but thought they only did good.
He was never taken by surprise
nor in a rush.
He never put off vital matters
nor became victim to worry or depression.
He didn't laugh to hide anger,
he was never over passionate
or ever frightened.

BOOK 1. MY TEACHERS

In my father
I saw mildness,
straightforwardness,
and the shunning of honors.
He loved work and perseverance.
He listened with all ears,
openly and attentively,
to anyone who came into
his presence
for the common good.
His understanding was based
on experience.
He knew how to choose between
vigorous action,
and simply doing nothing.
He had overcome his passion
for boys too.[12]
He saw himself as not better than
anyone else.
He freed his friends from all obligation
to dine with him
if necessity forced them to do otherwise.

[12] P. B. Shelley in his Essay on Love explained that homoeroticism was prevalent in Ancient Greek (and Roman) society because the women were largely uneducated and confined to domesticity. The male youths, however, were well educated and trained in athletic sports to conform to the idea of harmonious beauty, and often became more attractive than the women. This is also George Fuerstein's interpretation in 'Sacred Sexuality'. He says this led to bisexuality in ancient Greece (and Rome). Marcus Aurelius denounces this as an aberration and is proud of his father for having given up the vice.

Even when he went abroad, he freed
them accordingly from dutiful letter writing.
He carefully inquired in all
matters worthy of inquiry.
He was persistent, keen, and
never stopped at examining the mere surface
appearance.
He strived to delve deeper behind the illusion of life
into the "Thing in Itself."
His way was to help friends,
not be bored by them,
nor overdo his affections.
He was satisfied with whatever comes
and prized above all to be cheerful
and never down in the dumps,
and be on the watch for what was on
the way.
He would look after the smallest
member of society
without showing off.
But to stop immediately if there was
false applause or any hint of flattery.
He watched over all matters
that needed attention
for the common welfare of Rome.
He was careful with money,
and patient to suffer criticism

BOOK I. MY TEACHERS

for prudence.
He talked easily,
He was never
harsh,
violent,
or unyielding.
He examined all affairs
thoroughly
without confusion.
Like Socrates
he could abstain
or enjoy
those pleasures
which many were too weak
to refrain from
without excess.

17. Thank the Gods
    I came from a good family
    And I was no longer
    brought up
    by my grandfather's
    mistress
    and preserved the flower
    of my youth
    without wasting my virility
    and never committed

any excessive sexual deeds
I would later regret.
Finally I thank the Gods
for my affectionate,
obedient, simple wife,
my fine children,
and in philosophic matters
never to be misled by false charismatic teachers.
I am most grateful for all theses benefits
to the Gods.

BOOK II. RESOLUTIONS

1. I start each new day
    by resolving
    that whomever I meet
    even if they are busybodies
    pompous idiots,
    liars,
    or antisocial ingrates,
    that I will not be hurt
    or angered by them,
    but cooperate as best I can
    if it's for the common weal.
    To obstruct one another
    is against our natural instinct for "goodwill."

2. What we are
    is a little flesh,
    blood, breath, bones,
    sperm,
    and the power of Reason.
    So throw away trivial distracting
    books!
    Remember in old age
    to use the power of Reason
    and no longer be yanked
    like a puppet, to do hostile acts.
    Welcome all that happens,
    and never ever fear the future.

BOOK II. RESOLUTIONS

3. All that happens comes
    from Divine Providence.
    Everything has its place,
    it flows from the Source of Creation.
    Linked to what is necessary
    for the good of universal
    harmony and balance.
    I am part of that Universe
    so all that happens
    is to be wholeheartedly
    accepted.
    Change is inevitable,
    so I am happy.
    If death comes,
    I greet it with good grace
    and gratitude for the life
    I have been granted.

4. Think how many times
    you postponed things
    which the Gods have given
    you a chance to do.
    Realize the nature of this
    Universe
    and remember your time here
    is very short.
    So work for your "Enlightenment"

while you have the chance
or the possibility may vanish for ever.

5. Do every deed
    with dignity
    in a spirit of freedom, love,
    and justice
    as if it was your last.
    Renounce carelessness,
    irrationality,
    hypocrisy,
    egotism, and
    discontent with "what is."
    The Gods require nothing
    more than this
    I assure you.

7. If distracted by worry
    spare yourself space
    for quietness.
    Meditate on what is good
    and rein in restlessness.
    Don't over indulge
    in business activities
    which lack any
    needful purpose.

BOOK II. RESOLUTIONS

8. Failing to watch another's mind
does not always end in sorrow
but failing to watch
one's own thoughts
could be disastrous!

11. Remember you may die
at any moment
so regulate your life accordingly.

12. Notice everything dies
sooner or later.
We should be aware of
the power of the senses,
how strong they are
yet how fleeting.
We should study the true value
of those whose opinions
have gained them good reputations.
We should study the
inevitability of death
and recollect that we are
connected
to the Source of all being
and Creation
so there is nothing ever to fear.

13. Nothing is worse
    than the man of idle
    curiosity spying on others
    without attending to
    the "willfulness" within
    his own consciousness.
    One should reverence this force,
    keeping it free from lust,
    carelessness,
    and dissatisfaction with
    what inevitably must happen.
    What comes from the providential
    Source of Creation
    should be honored.
    Deeds of men and women
    are dear to us by reason
    of our common humanity.
    And the ignorant move us
    to compassion.
    Not to see the difference
    between the rational and the irrational
    is as bad as not being
    able to see
    the difference
    between black and white
    or gold and a pebble.

BOOK II. RESOLUTIONS

14. Even if you were to live
for thousands of years,
remember the only life you
really have
is the one given to you now.
The present moment is the only one
there is,
and the only one you can
truly lose.
The past is memory,
the future an idea.

15. Never forget, that all
that is said and written
is merely opinion.
Just get out of it what
you feel to be true.

16. Finally do not make
your soul a bitter cancer
by rebelling against
the inevitable circumstances
of your God-given life.
Never ever reject a fellow human
for being malicious
or acting with anger.
Do not be overpowered by

either pain or pleasure.
Do not be insincere or lie.
Do not act aimlessly or
thoughtlessly
without weighing up all the
consequences,
whether right or wrong,
like an able Judge.
Follow reason and always be
law abiding.

17. Remember in human life,
time is only a point,
in the mind.
Your substance is in constant
flux,
most perceptions are dull,
all is perishing,
the spirit is in a whirl,
the future difficult to foresee,
and fame has no discrimination,
she's a bitch goddess.
The body is like a river
in constant process.
The spirit is in a dream-like state.
Life is a struggle
and ends in oblivion.

BOOK II ◆ RESOLUTIONS

So what will guide us?
I answer unequivocally –
Philosophy!
So keep your "will" free
from violence,
superior to pain and pleasure.
Never drift aimlessly
nor hypocritically,
but accepting all that
happens wholeheartedly
with a big yea-say!
Await death cheerfully
so the elements may be dissolved
and consciousness
return to its Source.
Nothing is ever wrong if it follows
the "Nature of Things."

BOOK III. REFLECTIONS

4. Do not worry about the affairs of others,
   wasting away
   the life and energy you have left.
   Rather give your attention
   to something useful
   that you really enjoy.
   Let your thoughts be
   plain,
   simple,
   benevolent,
   wise,
   and friendly.

5. Work with full attention,
   without too many words
   or busy busyness.
   Let the God within your heart
   be your guardian,
   your intuition.
   Be cheerful and Self-reliant,
   not dependent on others for consolation.

6. If you find anything better
   in life than
   justice,
   faith,
   bravery,

BOOK III. REFLECTIONS

moderation
then turn to it with all
your might, and enjoy it.
But if nothing appears to be superior
to the God immanent in your heart,
impartially watching over you,
then give place to nothing else
like power which corrupts,
or lustful excess of pleasure.
It is better to act as a rational
human being than as an animal.
Keep judgment without pride
and make inquiry by a logical method.

7. Never break a promise,
    lose your self-respect,
    hate anyone,
    be over suspicious,
    swear,
    act hypocritically,
    desire forbidden fruit.
    Prefer your own intelligence
    and the rational "will" within,
    worship its excellence.
    Act no tragedies or melodramas,
    never groan, whinge, or moan.
    Do not seek too much solitude

or too much company.
Live without pursuing life
or flying from it.
Surrender care and anxiety,
for even if death comes quickly,
then leave decently, in good order.

8. In an austere, pure mind
    there will be no corruption,
    nothing servile,
    affected,
    bound,
    nor indifferent.
    Nothing that is worthy
    of blame,
    no skeletons in the cupboard.

11. Ponder on the definition
    of inner conflict,
    of anything presented
    to the senses,
    so as to see distinctly
    its substance,
    its true nature,
    its nakedness,
    its wholeness,
    and its value,

its use,
its reference
to man and the whole;
and the virtue
I need with
respect to it.
Then see how it is
composed
and how it will be
dissolved.
This lifts the mind,
out of its willfulness.
One should reflect,
all comes from God, the Source of
Creation,
and is now displayed
as a great tapestry
by the spinning jenny
of destiny on the loom of space and time.
Note it points to invisible archetypal
ideas or forms of the wonderful weaver,
of which this life is but a shadow play,
as the great Socrates revealed to Plato.

12. If one works
    at that presented
    to the senses,

following reason
seriously,
vigorously,
calmly,
rigorously,
undistracted,
keeping your divine essence
pure, clear,
expecting nothing,
fearing nothing,
satisfied with what comes,
guarding heroic truth
in the words one speaks
you shall be very happy
beyond any doubt.

13. As surgeons
    always have scalpels poised
    when needed
    so have principled scrutiny ready
    for the understanding
    of objects
    divine and man-made.

14. Be ready to
    to do anything
    even the smallest deed

to reconnect the link
between one's human essence
and the divine.
Nothing can be done really well
without this reconnection.

16. Let us look at
the meaning
of body,
soul,
intelligence.
To the body belongs sensation.
To the soul,
appetites of desire,
to the intelligence,
principles of reason.
To judge impressions
of forms
by their appearances alone
is animal.

BOOK IV · MEDITATIONS

1. One's divine inner ruler
    adapts quickly to "what is"
    and acts appropriately.
    Like a flame she licks
    whatever is thrown upon her,
    waxes higher, and consumes
    all in her path.

3. Common people seek
    glamorous retreats
    country mansions,
    villas by the sea,
    lodges in the mountains,
    but it is all unnecessary,
    as it is in thy power
    whenever one wishes
    to retire into one's own Self.
    Tranquility is the good
    ordering of the mind,
    the power to turn inward
    and rest in the Self.
    Constantly refresh and
    renew your spirits
    this way.
    To be pulled by the
    strings of desire alone
    belongs to wild beasts.

BOOK IV. MEDITATIONS

The good man and woman is ever happy
with whatever happens,
and with their destiny,
and vow not to pollute
the divinity latent in
their breasts,
nor disturb it by a host
of images,
but to keep the brain calm,
quiet, serene,
following the divine impulse
obediently.
Never denying Truth or Justice.
They are never angry
with those who doubt their integrity,
they are reconciled to their allotted portion
and rejoice in it swiftly,
letting go softly and gladly
when once the attention
has recognized its Self
and knows its own power.
Then it no longer needs
to be involved
with bodily ailments
but can be detached
from pain and enter
into it to dissolve it.

BOOK IV. MEDITATIONS

If the desire for fame
possesses you
then remember well how all
reputations are soon
forgotten.
And notice that infinity
lies each side of the present
moment.
The emptiness of flattery
and the changeability
of flatterers,
and the narrowness
of the space
in which all this happens,
flies away like a swallow in winter.
The whole earth is a point
in space and time
and your dwelling is only a
microdot in that.
Question one's discontent
with men's wickedness?
Remember that rational beings
exist for one another.
To tolerate is part of justice.
Men often do wrong against their best intent
but are forced by necessity,
thinking their acts are justified.

BOOK IV. MEDITATIONS

But remember that after enmity,
suspicion,
hatred,
war,
they are all stretched dead
and quiet at last,
rotting under the earth.
If you are dissatisfied
with your destiny
then also remember
either there is a providence
or it is just a random mix of atoms;
but consider the fact
that the world is one great
community.
If the sickness of body
worries you,
remember again that
thoughts mix with breath.
Finally remember
to withdraw into your Self
and never strain,
feel free,
look at the world as one of its
rational citizens.
The two important rules
are that events

cannot hurt the soul
as they are external,
our worries come from
our own thoughts
and opinions about them.
The second is that
everything changes
and soon passes away and dies.
Remember again how much
change
you've already witnessed.
The Universe is a great
transformation of energies.
Life is our mere opinion about it.

4. The power of thought,
reason, and intellect
are common to all men and
women as rational beings.
This reason directs
us how to act
and how not to act.
Then there is a common law
which makes us fellow citizens
of the world.
Just as my earthly
body is given to me from Earth

BOOK IV. MEDITATIONS

and my bodily fluids
from water,
my life force
comes from the Source
as does my brain.

5. Death like birth
    is a mystery of nature.
    First a composition from the
    elements,
    and then a decomposition from
    them.
    This is conformable to
    Nature
    and not opposed to our
    rational understanding.

6. Men act as they do
    inevitably,
    just as a fig tree must
    give us precious juice,
    but shortly I, he, and
    you shall be dead
    and our names forgotten,
    the fig tree flourishes
    for a while.

BOOK IV. MEDITATIONS

7. Remove your opinion
    and so is the complaint
    "I have been hurt"
    taken away,
    the hurt has vanished.
    So let go of opinions – they are so relative.

10. Everything which happens
    happens perfectly,
    it comes from the Source of Creation.

12. A man should have
    two guides at hand.
    Firstly only to perform
    what the ruling faculty
    of reason may suggest,
    secondly to change the view
    of any who oppose such wisdom.

13. Have you reason?
    I have!
    Why don't you use it?
    It does its own work
    what more do you want?

14. You exist as a minute part
    of a great whole.

BOOK IV . MEDITATIONS

You will eventually
disappear in that
which gave you life —
Consciousness.
You will be received back
into its
root principle
by transmigration.

15. There are many sticks
of frankincense
on the same altar.
One burns out first,
one later.
It makes no difference,
all bear their own fragrant perfume.

16. In ten days time
you will seem a God
to those who are now
bestial like apes
if you return to your
principles and respect for Reason.

17. Don't act as if you
were going to live
for ten thousand years.

Death hangs over you
like a heavy cloud.
While you live,
and it is in your power,
simply, be on the side of the good.

18. To avoid trouble
do not look to find
fault
with your neighbor's deeds
but only with your own.
A good man does not
criticize the depraved
morals of others;
rather he pursues the straight
line of goodness as an arrow
pursues its target,
as an excellent example.

20. All "that is" in every way
is beautiful,
like a red, red rose
is beautiful in itself,
and perfect in itself.
That which is truly
beautiful
has no need of any addition.

BOOK IV . MEDITATIONS

Praise is unnecessary.
Is an emerald made worse
if it is not praised
for its greenness?
Or gold for its aura,
ivory for its whiteness,
the cochineal dye for its purple,
the lyre for its vibration,
a tiny steel knife for its sharpness,
a lily for its glory,
a hydrangea bush for its blueness;
are they worse off
if no one flatters them?

21. If souls survive death,
how does the air contain them?
Infinitely.
You might as well ask
how the earth
finds room for all the
bodies
rotting in it, since
time immemorial?
The souls, after resting,
transmigrate
and return to their Source

BOOK IV. MEDITATIONS

so fresh souls
may return to play a part
in life's great melodrama.
Then think of all the animals
daily eaten by humans
and other beasts.
A great number are digested
and buried in the stomach
until excreted back to the Mother
earth.
So the earth recycles her bodies
and more are born into
flesh, blood, and life force
from the same soil.
So the conclusion is to
see clearly
the distinction between
matter,
spirit,
and their cause.

22. Do not be whirled
    about like a top on a string
    but in your every movement
    respect Justice,
    and with every impression

BOOK IV. MEDITATIONS

received through the senses
keep your power of comprehension
and understanding.

23. Everything harmonizes
with me
which harmonizes with
thee, oh Universe!
Nothing for me is too
early
or too late;
all in due time arrives.
All is luscious fruit for me
which the trees in their
seasons bring!
Oh nature,
from thee comes all things,
to thee all returns.
This is a dear orchard of
God.

24. To be calm, serene,
tranquil,
unstressed,
do not take on too much.
Only do what is

necessary
and as required.
To do things well
do only a few.
There will be more leisure
and less strain and
anxiety.
Question whether what
you are doing now
is truly necessary or not?
This applies also to
unnecessary thoughts,
which are the fathers of
unnecessary deeds.

25. Try out living a
virtuous life;
see how it suits you?
Thus is a man satisfied
with his portion
from the whole,
and happy with his just deeds
and enjoys a well-wishing temperament.

26. You have seen something
unpleasant, nasty,

BOOK IV · MEDITATIONS

instead look at this.
Your role is to be
serene,
sincere,
simple.
If someone is doing wrong,
the wrong lies within him.
Has this happened to you?
Note well that from the source of the
apparent Universe
from the beginning
all that happens
has been apportioned
and spun out for you.
Remember – life is short;
you must turn to
advantage
the present moment
by the help of Reason and
Justice.
Be sober in your "letting go."

27. Either the Universe is well
ordered
or random chaos?
But it is still a Universe.

BOOK IV. MEDITATIONS

But if there is order in
you
then there cannot be disorder
in the All.

28. A black character is
    stubborn, bestial, infantile,
    animal, stupid, fraudulent,
    depraved, scurrilous, and tyrannical.

29. He is a stranger to
    this Universe
    who is ignorant of "what is" there
    and "what is" going on in her.
    He is a runaway from
    reason,
    he is blind,
    blinkering the eyes of understanding.
    He is poor
    who is dependent on others
    and does not provide
    for himself or herself
    what is useful for life.
    He is a cancer in the
    Universe
    who separates himself

BOOK IV. MEDITATIONS

from his rational sense,
by being displeased and
critical of everything around him.

31. Love the skill
which you have learned
and be happy with it.
Pass through life
like one who has trusted
the Gods with all his
heart, soul, and might,
making yourself neither
a tyrant or slave of
anybody.

32. In the times of Vespasian
you saw
folks marrying,
procreating,
bringing up children,
being ill,
dying,
fighting,
celebrating,
shopping,
farming,

BOOK IV. MEDITATIONS

flattering,
being arrogant,
obstinate,
suspicious,
plotting,
cursing,
grumbling,
loving,
hoarding money,
seeking fame and power.
Well, now, none of this
melodrama exists,
they are all dead.
In ancient times
it was the same too.
Their lives have also gone,
as have all epochs
and ancient nations.
Similarly recall
those you know
who fritter their time away
on endless idle distractions.
If due attention is given to
what is needed
you will not be unhappy.
So welcome everything that happens

BOOK IV . MEDITATIONS

and if that is too hard
then welcome your inability
to welcome it.

34. Surrender to Clotho,[14]
allowing her to spin your
thread into whatever fancy clothes
she pleases.

35. All is only for a day,
that which remembers,
and that which is remembered.

36. Recollect always,
everything takes place through
change
and this Universe loves
nothing so much
as to change "what is"
and to create new things.
All that exists
is the seed
of what shall be.

[14] One of the fates.

BOOK IV . MEDITATIONS

38. Examine men and women's
    ruling principles –
    even Sages,
    what do they avoid and
    what do they seek?

39. Where does evil come from?
    To you, not from the mind of another
    nor from the changes and
    moods of your body;
    then from where?
    From that part of yourself
    which consists in the
    forming of opinions about what is evil.
    Refuse its judgments and
    all is well.
    Even if the poor soul
    nearest to you is cut, burned,
    rots, or whatever,
    let the part which forms
    opinions shut up.
    Let it only judge that
    nothing is either good or bad
    but thinking
    it is bad or good.[15]

[15] An idea found in Shakespeare's Hamlet.

BOOK IV. MEDITATIONS

For anything that happens
to men comes impersonally
whether they live according to
the rules of Nature or not.

40. See the Universe
as one living being,
with one substance,
one soul.
Notice how everything
refers to the perception
of this one living being
and how all acts with
one movement
and how all things work
together as the causes of
all things which exist.
Notice the continuous
spinning of the thread
and the structure of the web.

41. You are a little soul
carrying a corpse
as Epictetus said.

49. Be like the rock
against which rough waves

break
yet it stands solid
and tames the rage
of the waves around it.
I have not been created
just to lie asleep
in my pyjamas
to keep warm.
No!
Am I unwilling to play
the part
of an intelligent human being?
Even the ants, flies, mosquitoes,
tigers, baboons, fish,
the whole zoo,
play their part.
Why should I shirk?
It is necessary to rest too.
Nature has fixed bounds
to eating,
drinking,
sex
yet sometimes one advances beyond
these bounds.
Why not – are you not a probing
experimental human being?
Love your nature and respect

your will.
The will comes from the Source
at the level of the numinous it is free,
but at the level of the
phenomenal it is blind and
bound.
It is only tamed by reason,
and philosophic understanding,
so remember on every occasion
which leads you to anguish,
to apply this balm.
This is not a misfortune
which has happened
for to be able to bear it nobly
is very good fortune.

51. Always take the shortcut,
the way of Nature,
with conformity to sound
reasoning principles.
This frees men and women
from sorrow
and strife,
artificiality
and ostentation.

BOOK V. PONDERINGS

1. In the morning
   when you arise
   from the dream of sleep
   to the dream of life
   let this thought be the first one present;
   I am waking up
   to the way of a rational human being.

4. I advance through life's events
   according to my nature
   until I collapse and die,
   breathe out my last breath
   back into the Source
   from where I originally came.
   I shall rest in dear Mother Earth
   from which my
   father shed his seed and
   impregnated my essence,
   hidden in my own mother's sacred womb.
   And she it was who gave me milk,
   from her fulsome breasts.
   Divine providence
   has given me every day
   adequate food and drink
   which grants me a strong life,
   even when I abuse it, alas.

BOOK V. PONDERINGS

5. You may feel you
are not perfect,
quick – wise – all the time,
instead, I advise, you
cultivate the following virtues
sincerity, earnestness,
dignity, contentment,
industriousness, love,
sobriety, generosity.
Avoid grumbling and complaining.
Be
considerate,
frank,
temperate in speech,
authoritative, compassionate,
grateful.
See how many virtues
are immediately available,
yet you still fail to hit the mark.
Instead
you murmur,
are mean,
flatter,
complain,
crawl,
show off,
fidget.

BOOK V . PONDERINGS

You could have been saved
from these perils years ago.
So instead of being slow
and dull
you must try rather harder than
rejoicing in your dullness.

6. Some men and women,
    if they perform a good deed
    for another
    expect a reward.
    Some do not expect this,
    but in their minds
    think their friend should
    be oh, so grateful.
    Some do not expect
    any reward nor
    hold any expectation in mind.
    They are like the
    vine which bears luscious grapes,
    but seeks nothing else
    in return.
    Just as the horse after
    running a race,
    a dog who has tracked
    his game,
    a bee when it has made

its honey,
so should a man or woman be after work.
Virtue is its own reward.

8. A doctor prescribes
    to this man horse-riding
    or cold water baths
    or walking shoeless on fire,
    so the Universe justly
    prescribes suffering.
    It is suitable for one's destiny.
    So we accept everything
    that happens gladly,
    it comes from the Source
    of the Universe,
    and is in its way perfect.
    If you cannot accept wholeheartedly
    "what is"
    for some reason
    then at least accept your
    non-acceptance.

9. Do not be discouraged
    by failure to live rightly.
    Try again.
    What is more agreeable
    than acting wisely?

10. Truth is veiled
    in obscurity.
    To many philosophers,
    and even to the Stoics,
    all agreements are changeable.
    Show me the man or woman
    who never changes!
    Objects are short lived
    and generally worthless,
    any wretch, whore, or
    robber may own them.
    As for morals, they are dark,
    in flux,
    and relative.
    But rest in the truth
    that nothing can happen
    to me
    which is not conformable
    to the Nature of the Universe,
    and I cannot act against
    God's will if it is not permitted.

11. What am I doing now?
    I must often ask this
    question and inquire
    what is present in me
    at this moment?

BOOK V. PONDERINGS

This is called my ruling
principle;
I ask,
and whose thoughts do
I have now?
A child's,
a youth's,
a weak woman's,
a tyrant's,
a dog's, a cat's,
or a wild beast's?

12. What appears to be good
to the majority?
If they prefer such "goods"
as prudence,
temperance,
justice,
courage,
they would not have thought
they were worthwhile.
Can any virtue
be disharmonious
with the Universe?
If the people share
vulgar notions
they will see the old joke

BOOK V. PONDERINGS

of there being too many
"goods."
The majority share values
and are cautious
about too much wealth,
luxury, and fame.
So now the test.
Ask yourself
whether we do right
to think of so many things as "good."
If our mental picture is
"the owner of so many
goods,"
one has not even space to
ease oneself.

13. I am made up
of form and matter;
neither can pass away
into nothing
any more than
they can come from nothing.
So every part of me
one day
will be refashioned
by a process
of transmigration

BOOK V. PONDERINGS

into another place
in space and time
to infinity.

14. Reason and reasoning,
    that is Philosophy,
    are powers sufficient
    unto themselves and their works.
    They move from their own first principle
    and progress to their end.
    This is why acts proceeding from reason
    are called "right acts."

16. As are thy habitual
    thoughts,
    such is the character of
    your mind.
    The soul is dyed by
    thoughts.
    Dye it then with noble thoughts
    such as these.
    Firstly, wherever a man
    lives, there he can live well,
    even in a palace,
    or a prison.
    Secondly, the cause of
    each thing's development

points to its final end.
Thirdly, the chief good
of a rational being
is friendship with neighbors.
Friendship is a purpose
behind creation.
Fourthly, while the lower
exist for the higher,
the higher exist for one another.
While the animate is higher
than the inanimate
the rational is higher still.

17. To pursue the unattainable
is insanity.

19. Outward things cannot
affect the Self.
They know no way into it,
they are powerless to sway or move it.
It is Self-moving;
it has its own Self-approved
standards.
To them it refers all its experience.

20. The mind converts
and changes

BOOK V. PONDERINGS

every obstacle to its
action
as an aid.
We high-jump over the next
obstacle
and then we are better
equipped
to jump over the next.
There is no situation
presented to the enlightened
man with which he cannot cope.
He turns stumbling blocks
into stepping stones!

23. Think of the high speed
with which things
pass by and disappear,
like a chariot
at the races.
Substance is like a fast flowing river
in continual flood;
nothing ever stands still,
even if it appears to do so.
The past is a boundless
abyss,
dangerous to dwell on,
and the future unknown,

a perilous peak to imagine.
So stay in present time,
here and now
in the eternal now
feel "I AM"
consciousness, awareness, peace.
Only fools, have pity on them,
are plagued by the miserableness
of the past,
or fear of the future.
Help them if you have
the capacity,
or they will fall into the abyss.

24. Think of the whole
Universe
of which you are a tiny
minute portion
and of universal infinity
of which a short moment
has been given to you,
all of which is fixed
by the hand of destiny.[16]

---

[16] This verse recalls the verse in Omar Khayyam: The moving finger writes "and, having writ, moves on. Not all thy piety nor wit, shall lure it back to cancel half a line, nor all thy tears wash out a word of it." (Fitzgerald Transl.)

BOOK V. PONDERINGS

26. Let the Soul which
    leads and rules
    understand through
    sensations of pleasure or pain,
    whether ecstatic bliss
    or chronic bodily suffering.
    Do not resist, but welcome,
    what comes and don't add
    to it by the opinion that
    this is good, wonderful,
    this is bad, terrible.

27. Dwell with the Gods;
    this is best done
    by accepting all
    they give to you
    in accordance with
    their Will,
    making it your Will too.
    Your guardian, and guide,
    is a portion of the Gods
    from the Gods.
    This is every man and
    woman's reasoning,
    understanding, and experience,
    unless they are blind.

28. Are you angry with your
    brother and sister
    when their armpits stink?
    Or bear bad breath and fart?
    What good will being angry do?
    He or she has bad breath,
    foul smelling armpits and he or she farts.
    So what?
    It is an emanation
    on a subtle level from Source
    so accept, enjoy, it is not
    so bad,
    subtly aromatic, perhaps?
    If he or she has Reason
    he or she will control these features
    out of compassion for his or her fellows
    so there is no problem, as they say.

31. How have you behaved
    to the Gods,
    parents,
    brothers and sisters,
    children,
    teachers,
    friends,
    relations?

BOOK V. PONDERINGS

Can you honestly say
you "have never wronged a
man or woman in deed or word."
And remember all you've
been through,
all you've endured,
all the beauty you've seen,
all the pains and pleasures
you've resisted or enjoyed,
how much has been honorable
and how much disgraceful
and to how many fellows
have you been full of ill will
and to whom you have been kind?

32. Why do the ignorant
and unskilled
disturb the wise and skilled?
Because the Soul who
has skill and wisdom
knows reasons for causes
and effects
and that power which sustains
all matter,
and through time, governs
the Universe.

The ignorant and unskilled
do not know this.

33. Soon you'll be burned to ashes
and end up a skeleton;
you'll be devoured by worms.
Nameless forever,
not even a sound or echo
of a name will remain;
all that is valued
will have been found to be empty,
pointless, and trifling.
Just as puppies bite
each other
and little children quarrel
then weep.
Faith, modesty, and justice
have fled
back up to the heavens from the
widespread earth.
Why do you value this place
so much?
The objects of your senses
are quickly changed
and never stand still.
The organs of perception are dull

BOOK V. PONDERINGS

and easily receive false
impressions.
Even to have a good reputation
means very little.
Instead wait, calmly, serenely,
tranquilly for your death.
And until your time arrives
what is needed?
To respect the Gods,
do good to men,
be tolerant,
and self-restrained.
But to everything beyond the limits
of thy weak flesh and breath,
remember nothing is yours,
nor in your power.

34. You can live your life
in an even flow of happiness.
If you do, think and
act correctly.
All right actions are
common.
To the inner essence of the divine
in all men and women.

36. Do not be misled by
    appearances.
    Assist all according
    to ability and their capacity
    to receive help.
    Good fortune is a
    good disposition,
    good feelings, good deeds,
    and a sharp intellect.

BOOK VI. APHORISMS

1. Universal matter
   obeys natural laws
   and that which governs all
   is benign.
   All things are created
   then perfected
   according to the powers of Reason.

2. Don't be concerned
   about being hot or cold
   as long as you are
   doing your duty,
   or whether you are drowsy
   or keenly awake;
   or well spoken about
   or blamed
   and whether dying
   or simply living.
   It is adequate just
   to do excellently
   whatever task we have
   in hand.

3. Turn the mind within
   and gaze intensely,
   let nothing escape your
   inner attention.

4. Everything is destined
to change
and will be shortly reduced
to vapor.
All substance is one
and will be returned
to the Source.

8. The ruling principle
is that which awakens
and then turns in on itself
making itself such as it wills to be.
Everything which happens
appears to itself as it wills.[17]

11. When circumstances
force you to be disturbed,
quickly return to your Self;
you will master harmony
by continuous Self recollection.

12. If you loved a stepmother
and your mother
at the same time

[17] This verse anticipates the nineteenth-century German transcendental philosophies of
Kant, Schopenhauer, Nietzsche, Hegel, Fichte, Schelling, Schlegel, etc. when they were
preoccupied with the nature of the Will and the "thing in itself."

you would be dutiful
to your stepmother
but constantly return
to your real mother.
So let the Court-life be your stepmother
and philosophy be your mother.
Return to philosophy often
and rest in her.
In the Court whomever you meet
is tolerable, and you are to them.

13. When dining
    we often think
    that dead body
    we attack with knife and fork
    was only a cow munching grass,
    a salmon leaping in the stream,
    a pheasant flying in the fields,
    a pig wallowing in the trough,
    and this delicious vintage ruby wine
    is only grape juice,
    and my purple robe
    just sheep's wool
    dyed with cochineal.
    Sex is only a rubbing of
    members together,
    and discharges follow.

BOOK VI. APHORISMS

Politicians are egotists
so trouble follows their acts.
So we see the actual
quality
and root of things.
This is how we should
perceive life.
Strip things naked
to their core
and forget the exalted
words which surround them;
the outward glitter
often perverts common sense
and reason;
and paradoxically
when you are sure
you are employed doing
things worth pain
they cheat you the most.

14. Most objects
    which the mob likes
    are of a mundane
    kind,
    held together by natural cohesion
    such as gray stone,
    brown wood,

fig trees,
grape-vines,
olive trees;
but those who have more
rational sense,
prefer things held together
by a living principle,
such as flocks of sheep,
herds of cattle,
squadrons of birds,
orchards of apples.
But those more instructed
in philosophy and wisdom
aim at keeping their souls
conformable to Reason
and a happy social life.
He or she works best with those who
have similar interests.

15. Some things are rushing
    pell-mell into existence,
    others are rushing out.
    Motion and changes
    continually renew our world,
    just as time renews the ages.
    In this river on which there is
    no bank to rest,

BOOK VI. APHORISMS

what is there of the things
which rush which are
truly worthwhile?
It is just as if you should
fall in love
with a sparrow that flies
past,
but is now out of sight.
It is like respiration,
we inhale and exhale
from our first breath
at birth
we return it to the Source
from whence we drew it,
in the first place,
and so on until death.

17. Above and below,
all around,
the elements dance.
But the movement
of virtue
is not there.
It is found by diving into the heart
and advancing by
a path, happily and invisibly.

Trust that power which
knows the way.

20. In the gym,[18]
    pretend a man has
    scratched you
    or hit you on the head.
    Well, we may not
    show offence,
    yet we are now on guard against him
    and avoid his presence.
    So in life we overlook
    many things
    like we do antagonists
    in the gym.
    It is in our power
    to get out of the way
    without suspicion or hatred.

28. Death is the end
    of the impressions
    which move the senses
    and the pulling of the puppet strings
    which move desire

---

[18] I have kept this verse as it illustrates the perils of the gymnasia in ancient Rome. Perhaps twenty-first-century health clubs are safer places?

BOOK VI. APHORISMS

and the random movement
of thoughts
and lusts of the flesh.

29. The soul should not
despair about death,
before the body does.

31. Return to sobriety
when you wake up
and see all that troubled
you were only dreams.
Now look at all about you
as keenly as you did in
your dreams.
Do not take delivery
of troublesome thoughts,
they are a poisonous beverage,
after all, life is only a
waking dream.

33. The work the hand does,
and that which the foot does,
are not against nature
as they do their own work.
The same with a man's

or woman's toil,
it is only evil if it is
against his better nature.

34. How extraordinary
are the pleasures
enjoyed by robbers,
parent and child murderers, dictators,
just think what they are.

35. Asia and Europe
form the corners of the
world.
All the sea is a drop
in the Universe.
Rome is but a clod of the whole.
The present time is but
a point in eternity.
All things are minute,
changeable,
perishable.
All things emerge from
the Source.
Even the lion's open jaws,
poisonous plants,
prickly thorns,

muddy sludge,
are results of something "other,"
so grand and beautiful.

37. To see the "all" of
the present moment
here and now
is to see "all" that
has eternally been
and all that shall be.
For the "all"
is a unity of substance
and form.

38. Frequently contemplate
the interconnection of all things
in the holistic Universe
and their inter-relationship.
All things have an amiable
correspondence with each other.
By reason of their contraction
and expansion
in movement,
there is an empathy that breathes
through them
and their essential unity.

39. Adjust to your destiny.
    Love all that happens,
    inwardly
    and outwardly,
    honestly,
    wholeheartedly.

42. We are all working for
    one end.
    Some with knowledge and
    purposes,
    others without them,
    they are like workers asleep.
    Heraclitus, I think, says they are
    hypnotized, unconscious
    cooperators with the cosmic whole.
    Men cooperate differently,
    even the fault-finders
    and opposers cooperate.
    The universal drama needs
    difficult men and women like these.
    You must look and see
    the kind of workman you are.
    Be used by the higher
    power for good,
    as an instrument.

But don't be a ridiculous clown
in the play, as Chrysippus
describes.

43. Does the sun do the
work of the rain?
Or does the great physician
Aesculapius the work of
the fruit bearing earth?
Each star is different,
yet they work together
harmoniously
for the common good.

48. When you wish to become
happier,
think of the virtues of others,
their right activity,
egolessness,
generosity,
kindness,
helpfulness,
gentleness,
gratitude,
affection,
warmth,
wisdom,

clarity.
Nothing delights us so much
as virtues
when shown in the behavior
of those around us.

53. Attend and listen
with great care
to what is said by
another.
Be in the speaker's mind;
it will affect him
and bring him to awareness
of his own speech.

54. Remember that what is not
good for the beehive in swarm
is not good for the bee either.

55. If sailors abuse the
captain,
or the patients their
doctors,
will they listen to any
wisdom?
How can the captain
secure their safety,

or the doctor their health
unless they follow his
advice?

57. To the jaundiced, honey
tastes bitter.
Those bitten by dogs
are fearful.
Why then am I angry?
Because a false opinion
has more power
than bile in the jaundiced
or the rabies in he who was bitten
by a dog.

58. No man can stop you
living according to the Reason
of your true, own Nature,
consciously aware and
peaceful.
Nothing will happen against
you because of the same Reason
of the universal true Nature.

59. What kind of persons
are those whom men and
women

desire to please?
And for what motives?
And by what deeds?
Time will soon cover up
all these strivings;
it has covered up
plenty already.

BOOK VII. ADVICE

1. Evil has often been seen,
   all history is filled with it,
   in ancient ages
   and in modern times,
   cities and houses are filled
   with it now.
   There is nothing new
   under the sun,
   everything is familiar and
   short lived.

2. How can our better principles die?
   Unless the impressions which
   support them are not kept alive
   and they are not fed.
   It is in your power
   to fan these principles into
   a blazing bonfire.
   I can always have a
   just opinion,
   so why am I disturbed?
   That which is external
   to my mind
   does not have to affect
   me
   nor do I need to have
   judgmental opinions

all the time.
Stand firm!
To recover your life is
within your power.
Take a fresh look at
events,
there is no situation on earth with
which you cannot deal
appropriately.

3. Consider the idle trivialities of
    shows,
    theaters,
    extravaganzas,
    grazing sheep,
    ruminating cattle,
    throwing javelins aimlessly,
    chucking bones at dogs,
    bread into fish-ponds.
    Watch the toil of the ant,
    he keeps running around like
    a frightened mouse,
    or puppets pulled by strings
    and all the same.
    It is only duty.
    In the midst of such nonsense
    it is necessary to show

good humor,
never proudly,
and to remember that every man
and woman
is worth as much as the things
with which I busy myself.

7. Never be ashamed to
accept help.
Be like a soldier in
battle.
If you are wounded
you need help
to mount the battlements.

8. Never worry about the future;
it is a waste of energy
and substance.
Meet whatever comes with equanimity
and the power of reason.
All shall be well,
I promise.

9. Everything is interconnected,
the bond is holy.
All has been coordinated
to combine for universal order,

BOOK VII. ADVICE

balance, and harmony.
There is one Universe
made of many objects,
one God who pervades all,
one substance,
one law,
one common Reason in intelligent
beings,
one truth.
There is also a perfection
in animals
which are from the same
Source
and participate in the great drama according
to their nature.

15. Whatever anyone says or
does
I must be good,
as this is my nature
as gold, emerald, and
the purple dye,
have their natures.
I must be like them
and keep my true color always.

16. The Reason
    is never frightened
    or causes pain.
    Let the body be careful
    that it avoids suffering,
    but if it suffers
    let it accept suffering.
    Embracing it wholeheartedly.
    This is a great cure.
    The soul feels fear
    and pain,
    but will avoid suffering by
    not forming opinions about it
    and keeping silent.

17. Happiness
    is a good spirit,
    so let negative imagination
    alone, like the bubonic plague,
    and cast it out abruptly.

18. Never fear change,
    everything has to change
    sooner or later.
    You cannot even take
    a hot bath
    unless the fuel undergoes

BOOK VII. ADVICE

a change.
You can't enjoy a good meal
unless the food undergoes
a change.
For yourself to change is
equally necessary
for the universal harmony;
it will bring it about
in its own good time.

19. Through the great universal
river,
as in a wild torrent,
all bodies are swept along,
by their natures united
and cooperating with the whole,
as parts of our body with
one another.
How many a Chrysippus,
how many a Socrates, how
many an Epictetus[19]
has the river of time
already drowned?
And this applies to every
man and thing equally.

[19] Great Greek philosophers.

22. Men even have the blessed
capacity
to love those who do evil against
them.
They realize that they are kinsmen
sharing the same ultimate consciousness,
awareness, and rationality,
even if displaced through ignorance
unintentionally.
They also perceive that sooner or later
we'll both die
and ultimately the so-called wrongdoer
has not injured your reason or sense
of justice[20]
or your ruling faculty one bit.
Bless him or her,
decide, oh friend, are you
predominantly on the side of
goodwill or not?
Most citizens are,
a few are not
and cause considerable trouble.
Such is the divine drama
In which we each play our
pre-ordained part.

[20] Marcus Aurelius often refers to Justice. By this he means the rights of the ordinary citizen against the tyranny of the State and wise judgment between conflicts involving citizens and a process against criminals intent on destabilising society.

BOOK VII. ADVICE

23. Come to terms with death;
    it is no hardship for your
    planetary body
    to be dissolved back into its source
    from where it came.
    Your emotional experiences and
    subtle leavings will
    transmigrate into another body,
    but your ego in the brain
    will die
    with its decomposition.
    You are not the owner of
    your life.
    Let him who owns it
    do what he likes
    with it,
    affirm his will,
    and be his slave – be free,
    be happy,
    meanwhile enjoy your place
    and enjoy your portion,
    That is His Will.

24. A scowling, frowning look
    is unnatural;
    it is often put on.

Good looks fade away,
frowning and scowling
could become a habit
and lead to ugliness.
It is against Reason and
common sense.

27. Think not of what
you have not got,
but be grateful for what
one has,
and of these select the best
and reflect how keenly
you would seek them
if you hadn't been given
them already.
But take care that,
being over pleased,
you may become proud
and egotistic
and overvalue these qualities,
worrying that you might
lose them, oh dear.

28. Retire into your Self.
The rational principle

BOOK VII. ADVICE

is happy
with this effort
and so gains peace.

29. Wipe out negative
imagination
and fantasy,
stop their string pulling.
Live in the present
moment,
the eternal here and
now!
Understand what is
happening to you
and to others.
Discriminate between
the form and
substance of everything.
Meditate on your last
hour.
It will bring you to the Self,
let the wrong done by
anyone
stay where it has been done,
don't carry it about in the mind
like a bundle of baggage.

31. Garland yourself
    with flowers
    of simplicity and
    modesty,
    and detachment
    from all that swings
    between virtue and vice.
    Love mankind,
    seek God,
    His law rules all.
    This is sufficient
    to remember.

35. From Plato
    the philosopher of
    evolved understanding,
    who had a vision of eternity
    and its substances,
    even he did not think
    a human life
    was in any way great.
    "It is not possible" he said.
    He did not think death
    to be an evil either.[21]

---

[21] Republic VI. 486.

BOOK VII. ADVICE

36. It is royally ennobling to do good
and then suffer abuse for it.

40. Life must be harvested
like the ripe ears
of golden corn,
one man is born
another dies,
so be it.

43. Do not wallow with others
in their greedy wanting.
Violent emotions are
to be shunned.

47. Look at the stars
in the heavens,
watch their courses,
as if you were moving
with them,
and consider their
elemental changes
into one another.
Such thoughts cleanse one
from the dirt of earthly life.

48. This is a grand thought
    of Plato's.
    He or she who discourses
    about mankind
    should contemplate
    earthly affairs
    as if he viewed them
    from a higher place.
    Watch their assemblies,
    armies
    farms,
    marriages,
    diplomacies,
    births,
    deaths,
    courts of justice,
    deserts,
    barbarian tribes,
    feasts,
    funerals,
    markets,
    a great mix of all
    things,
    an orderly combination
    of opposites,
    in balanced harmony.

BOOK VII. ADVICE

49. Look at history,
    such great changes
    of rulers.
    You may even foresee
    what will be.
    They will certainly
    be similar.
    They rarely deviate
    very much
    as egos are involved.
    If you have seen
    life clearly
    for forty years
    it is as good as
    for ten thousand.

50. That which has
    grown from the earth returns to
    the earth,
    but that which has
    sprung from heavenly seed
    returns to heaven.[22]

51. Will fancy food, drinks,
    cunning magic, and art,

---

[22] A quotation from Chrystippus by Euripedes.

turn the river's course
to escape from death?
The wind which the
Source has engendered
we must endure, and suffer
without complaint.[23]

52. A man may be expert
in defeating his opponent,
but let him be more unassuming,
more modest,
better disciplined,
to welcome all that happens
and more considerate of
his neighbor's faults.

55. Do not waste energy
trying to discover
other men and women's
ruling principles.
But look straight inside to see
what nature rules you.
Both are universal, and
your own,
they cause events

[23] From Chystippus by Euripedes, fragment 836.

BOOK VII. ADVICE

to happen.
The first principle
is usually the "social,"
the second is to
resist bodily inclinations
and not be overpowered
by the senses or animal desires.
The third is freedom from error.
And from being deceived
by the world of illusion.

57. Love all that happens
to you,
inside and out.
All is woven by the thread
of destiny.
What could be better?

59. Gaze steadily within,
there you find the
fountain of goodwill.
It will ever bubble
and sparkle
with refreshing clear
water,
but you must dig deep,

to find the well
from which it springs.

61. The art of life
    is more like that of
    the wrestler
    than the dancer.
    It must stand steady
    and firm
    to meet assaults
    which are often sudden
    and "out of the blue."

63. Every Soul, the philosopher says,
    is delivered of truth,
    justice,
    temperance, and
    benevolence
    against its will.[24]
    If you remember this
    you'll be more gentle
    towards others.

64. Take care not to
    feel against the animals

---

[24] The Will of Nature is a blind stirring, say the Stoics, unless tempered by Reason.

as they feel towards
mankind.

67. Nature has implanted
intelligence
in the mind
to give you the
power
to subject all your
tendencies
to Reason.
It is possible to be a
God-Man
and unrecognizable
to others.
Very little is needed
to live a happy life.
Despair of dry intellectual
hair-splitting
or mere knowledge of
the natural sciences
but hope and trust in
being free,
egoless,
amiable,
and obedient to God's Will.

68. It is within your power
to be free and at peace
within your Self
even if the whole world
condemns you,
and wild beasts attack you.
In all that, nothing
can stop the mind from
possessing itself,
from correctly judging
what is taking place
around one.
The present moment
is the here and now,
It is always an invitation
for reason, friendship, and awareness
to cooperate.
Such is the way of good
men and the Gods.
Nothing ever happens which
is irrelevant
to the man or woman
of goodwill.

71. It is easy to fly from
    one's own wickedness,
    but not so easy to fly from
    someone else's.

75. The nature of the whole
    was impelled to create
    a Universe,
    now all that comes into
    being
    does so by natural sequence,
    towards which the universal
    ruling impulse
    makes necessary for balance
    and harmony.
    Now throw that thought away.
    Instead just be happy to
    live the rest of your days
    as your true nature wills.
    Watch what it wills
    and let nothing else distract
    you from this aim
    for you have had experience
    already
    of many efforts without
    having found lasting happiness.
    Not in logical analysis,

nor wealth,
reputation,
sensual pleasure,
nor anywhere else.
Where is it then?
In doing what your true
Nature requires.
How do you do this?
Adopt principles which
relate to good and evil.
The good is which leads
you to be just, moderate,
and free.
The evil is that which takes
you in the opposite direction.
Remember this and you
will face many an ill
with tranquil serenity.
and ease.

BOOK VIII. MAXIMS

1. This meditation will
   remove the desire for shallow
   fame of name,
   the bitch goddess.
   Try as one might,
   it is not in your power
   to have lived your
   life from youth onwards
   like a true philosopher.
   It is plain you are far
   from this ideal.
   You have fallen into
   disorder in your inner states,
   your life plan contradicts
   it too.
   If now after reflection
   you have seen where the
   fault lies,
   throw that thought away.
   Instead just be happy to
   live the rest of your days
   as your true nature wills.
   Watch what it wills
   and let nothing else distract
   you from this aim,
   for you have had experience

already
of many efforts without
having found lasting happiness,
neither in logical analysis,
wealth,
reputation,
sensual pleasure,
nor anywhere else.
Where then?
In doing what your true
nature requires.
How do you do this?
Adopt principles which
relate to good and evil
The good is what leads
you to be just, moderate,
and free.
The evil is that which takes
you in the opposite direction.

2. On the occasion of
any deed
ask the question,
Do I regret it?
Shortly I will have
left the body
and all will have gone.

BOOK VIII. MAXIMS

What more do I seek?
If what I am now
doing
is the work of an intelligent,
rational human being
and, what is more, a
social being,
who under the supreme law
of the Divine will knows that all
is ordained and well.

3.   Alexander the Great,
     Galus, and Pompey[25]
     compared with
     Diogenes, Heraclitus,
     and Socrates[26]
     understood life,
     its causes, forms, and
     the nature of matter,
     and the ruling principles
     of these men were in tune
     with their inquiries.
     But as to the conquerors,
     what did they care about?
     Except for victory, war,

[25] Military generals.
[26] Philosophers.

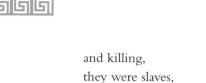

BOOK VIII. MAXIMS

and killing,
they were slaves,
callous about the value
of human life.

5. This is the chief principle.
    Never be perturbed,
    Disturbed, or frightened,
    for all things are of
    the way of universal law
    and in a short time you
    will be nobody,
    like the Emperors Hadrian
    and Augustus.
    Having decided on what
    is your chosen vocation
    fix your attention
    upon it.
    Love what you wish to do
    and love doing it.
    Remember it is your
    imperative, categorical duty
    to be on the side of the good
    and what nature asks,
    without turning aside or
    stumbling.
    Turn stumbling blocks

into stepping stones.
But let it be with a jovial
temperament,
with egolessness,
and without the dark red stain of
hypocrisy.

7. Be happy when
   things go well,
   when its thought
   consents to certain truth,
   and is sociably benevolent,
   controls its desiring and dislikes,
   when it is satisfied
   with whatever comes.

8. You may not have
   the time to read all the books
   of the wise,
   but you have time to
   check pride,
   to be above carnal pleasures,
   drunkenness,
   and bodily pain,
   to be above the drive for
   name and fame.
   And not to be angry

BOOK VIII. MAXIMS

with stupid ingrates,
but ever to care for
their welfare.

10. Repentance is only
self-reproof
for neglecting
something necessary.
The good is always
useful,
the perfect man cares
for that,
but he would never
repent for neglecting sensual
pleasures,
as they are of little good and addictive.

11. Great questions to ponder.
This thing, what is it in itself? [27]
What is its substance?
What is its matter?
What is its causal nature
or form?
What is its place in the Universe?
How long does it endure?

---

[27] This is the question that exercised Immanuel Kant and led to the metaphysical schools of
Schopenhauer, Bradley, etc.

BOOK VIII. MAXIMS

12. When you wake up
    with reluctance,
    remember it is your duty
    as a rational human being
    to participate in society
    for its betterment.

13. Constantly,
    when impressions strike the soul,
    question with the principles of
    physics, ethics and logic.

18. That which dies
    does not leave the
    Universe.
    It remains, changes,
    is dissolved into its elements,
    of the Universe and your Self.
    Suffer all these changes without
    complaint.

21. Turn the body
    inside out
    like a paper bag,
    and what will you see?
    When it grows old

what does it become?
and when it is diseased
what is it?
Excrement, blood, bone, sperm,
and rotting flesh.

24. Such as after bathing
   in blue water
   all filth appears,
   oil, sweat, dirt, and gunge,
   so is much of life,
   after bathing in the clear waters
   of the Self.

27. There are three
   significant relationships,
   first to one's own bodily form,
   secondly to the divine cause,
   from which all things
   emanate,
   thirdly to those whom
   you meet daily.

30. Address both the
   senate
   and every man or
   woman

of whatever station
appropriately,
not with affectation,
but affection,
in simple language.

32. It is thy imperative duty
    to order thy life well
    in each deed.
    If each act does its
    work,
    then rest contented.
    No one can prevent
    each act from having
    its effect.

33. Receive prosperity
    without pride
    as a gift
    and be ready to
    let it go.

34. If you've ever seen
    a hand cut off,
    or a foot, or a head,
    lying anywhere
    separate from its body,

BOOK VIII, MAXIMS

maybe you are doing
the same
by detaching yourself
from the natural unity
of oneness,
but it is in your power
to re-unite.
By remembering your Self,
the source of your own being,
consciousness, awareness,
God.
It is this grace that permits
You to return home.

36. Do not disturb
yourself
by musing on the
whole of your life.
Do not let thoughts
play havoc
by worrying about
what may happen,
and what may not happen,
but instead, ask yourself
the question,
what is there in this
that I cannot endure?

You will then discover
there is no situation
which may arise
that you cannot
deal with effectively.

38. If you can,
see keenly
with intensity,
look with attention,
discriminate wisely.
So speaks the philosopher.[28]

39. In the make up of
men and women,
rational animals,
I see no virtue
opposed to justice,
but there is a virtue
opposed to excess of sensuality
that is temperance.

40. If you remove that
false opinion
about yourself

[28] Crito, the Stoic.

BOOK VIII. MAXIMS

which causes pain
then you stand in safety.
As yourself "who am I?"
The Reason, you may reply.
No, you are not the Reason
so don't let the Reason
trouble itself;
you are consciousness
in which all takes place,
including Reason.
So if any part of you suffers,
let it have its own opinion
about itself
for what it's worth.

41. Hindrance to sense perception
is an evil to the animal nature
as is a hindrance to the
movement of desires.
But for a rational human being,
there are no hindrances
or impediments
neither fire, iron, or tyrant
can affect the Self
of pure consciousness – awareness
in harmony with the will of

the Source
by willing whatever happens
inside or out
on the screen of consciousness –
awareness.
It has been created as
a spherical mirror;
it remains a spherical mirror
for you to enjoy its reflections
in consciousness.

42. It is wicked to give
myself to pain
for I have never, ever
given pain to another.

43. Different events delight
different folk.
My delight is to keep
the ruling faculty of Rationality
sound and alert,
without rejecting my
fellow beings
or events in life,
but instead looking at
and receiving all

BOOK VIII. MAXIMS

with wholehearted
affirmation, gladly,
and loving all according
to their unique value.

44. Live in the present;
those who desire
posthumous fame
like the politicians
do not see that all
fades from memory
as today's red rose on
your mantelpiece.
Enjoy the perfume as
you may,
see it as a perfect
expression of divine beauty,
but it will fade away,
I assure you, with love.

45. Take me or throw me out
as you will,
but I shall keep my soul
tranquil and happy;
no change of place will
disturb me.
I am that I am,

linked to the Source of
my own being
for ever and ever,
so be it.
And you, my dear reader, are
in the same canoe
crossing to another shore,
of love, peace, and beauty.
Anchor in the Truth.
I welcome you as my
companion on the
great Odyssey.
Together we shall find the Golden Fleece.

46. Nothing can happen
    to any man
    which is not pre-ordained
    by the universal force
    and will.
    The future is already there,
    an ox suffers the fate of
    an ox.
    So does the vine,
    to be transformed into
    fine red wine;
    as the ox sires a cow,
    pulls a burden,

BOOK VIII. MAXIMS

or is served up as a
beef steak;
stones have their destiny
too
and strike politicians
between the eyebrows.
All is according to divine law.
Why complain?
Why explain?
You are a part of God;
the solution, to make you
happy,
is to will what He wills,
then all will be well,
you are in harmony with
the Universe
you fortunate man or
woman.
There is nothing on this
planet which you cannot
endure
and conquer,
even your inevitable death.

48. Remember
your ruling principle
of Rationality

is invincible!
When Self-collected,
if it does nothing to
resist "what is,"
the mind free from
passion
is a fortress,
so dive into the citadel
of your own heart for a true rest
and safe-keeping.

49. Comment nothing more
    to yourself
    than what first impressions
    report.
    Suppose you are told
    that a person
    spoke badly about you.
    This has been reported
    but by adding to it mentally
    you increase the hurt.
    Let it die away, being
    starved of thought and feeling.
    You are unaffected
    by praise or blame
    in the Self.

50. If a cucumber is bitter,
    throw it away,
    there are thorns on the path,
    turn aside.
    This is enough,
    do not add
    "oh dear, why were
    such things made
    in this world."
    You will be ridiculed
    by a man
    who knows Nature
    as you would by a
    carpenter or shoemaker
    if you find fault
    because you see
    shavings and cuttings
    on their workshop floors.
    True, they have places
    to throw these wastes,
    but universal Nature
    has no specific space
    for this need.
    Now the wonderful part
    of her art,
    that everything within
    her that decays and ages

she transforms back into
herself,
and makes new forms
out of these old ones.
So she doesn't require
new matter
nor a place to throw waste
away.
She is happy with her own
space,
her own matter,
her own art.
So should we rational
men and women be, too.

51. Do not be sluggish or
slothful in deeds,
nor in conversation aimless,
nor in thoughts, perverted
or wandering like a herd
of stampeding cattle.
Do not inwardly have
divisions,
nor be over elated in
outside events.
Do not be so busy as
to have no leisure.

Even if men kill you,
cut you up into little
pieces,
curse and spit on you,
it will not prevent your
Self from remaining
pure,
wise,
sober,
just,
untouched,
free.
If a man should curse
a spring from a pure mountain
stream,
it would still go on bubbling
with crystal clear water,
even if he throws clay
or dirt into it;
soon it will swiftly disperse even
that,
wash them out, and stay
unpolluted.
You can have such a
perpetual fountain,
and not only a well,
by linking your mind

to freedom,
the Source of your being,
Self, consciousness, awareness,
love, simplicity, and
egolessness.

52. He who does not
    understand
    what the Universe is
    does not know where he
    is either.

53. No longer be happy
    just with thy breathing
    acting in concert with
    the air,
    but let thy intelligence
    harmonize with the
    universal intelligence too.

55. Wickedness does no
    harm to the great Universe,
    it is unaffected.

57. The sun's rays are
    endlessly effused,
    one can see a single

BOOK VIII. MAXIMS

ray when one beam
enters a narrow nook
in an extended dark room.
Such should be our
understanding of understanding.
It should be an extension,
not an effusion,
but be single and enlighten
that which it strikes,
in the mind or in the world.
A body will lack light
If it does not welcome it
and understand it this way.

58. He who fears death
fears loss of sensation
or an unknown sensation
to come.
If one does not desire
or fear sensation
you will become
a different being
and live eternally.

60. An arrow can fly aimlessly,
so does the mind.
But when it is directed

on Self enquiry,
it moves straightforwardly right
onto its target.
Bulls-eye!

61. Enter into every man's
ruling principle
and let every man
enter into yours.

BOOK IX. WISDOM

1. Injustice is impiety,
   the liar is too,
   so is he who only
   seeks pleasure,
   who is cruel,
   and does not see inflicting
   pain as evil.
   But those who are in
   harmony with Nature
   have a neutral attitude
   toward pain and pleasure,
   death and life,
   good reputation and bad.
   They see that
   by some primal impulse
   of the Source of all being
   a chain of sequences
   inevitably follows,
   to create an ordered
   Universe
   in balanced harmony as
   a whole.

   It would be good for a
   man to die
   without having tasted
   lying,

BOOK IX. WISDOM

hypocrisy,
excessive luxury,
pride.
However, the next best
is to die when he has
had enough of such folly.
Fly from vice
like the bubonic plague,
it is a corrupt pestilence.

Do not despise death,
make friends with it,
it is Nature's will
and by willing what nature
wills
we are at peace and
harmony with her.
For great as it is to be
young,
or
aging,
or
mature,
to be a father,
a mother,
so also is death.
One should await

its arrival,
be ready
for the soul to fall out
of its jacket.
Beware of men who have
forgotten their own Selves;
one might say if I
was like that
"come quickly, death, lest
I too should forget my Self."

9. All which is earthly
    returns to earth,
    all liquids flow together
    as does the air,
    fire moves upward
    to its element.
    In animals we find herds,
    with bees swarms,
    with birds flocks,
    a power brings them together,
    unlike with stones and plants.
    But in rational animals,
    like men and women,
    there are states,
    societies,
    associations,

friendships,
families,
assemblies,
treaties,
armistices.
In the stars a unity exists,
in galaxies.
All finds its union,
naturally in the end,
so trust that power
which knows the way to unity.

11. If you can,
    correct by teaching
    wrongdoers,
    but if you cannot,
    be tolerant
    as the Gods are;
    they even help them to get
    health,
    wealth,
    reputation,
    so merciful are they.
    It is in your power too,
    so be forgiving.

12. Work not as one who is
    miserable,
    nor as one who should
    be pitied or admired,
    but direct your will
    to one single aim
    to put yourself on a course of rightful action
    and to be aware to check
    yourself
    as the social Reason needs.

13. Today I have rid myself
    of all inner disturbance!
    I saw clearly that it
    did not lie outside
    but inside as my
    own opinions.

14. Essentially, all things are the same,
    familiar in experience,
    transitory in time,
    worthless in the end.
    Everything now
    is just as it was in the time
    when we attended friends'
    funerals
    and then buried them, alas.

BOOK IX. WISDOM

15. Things, objects, thoughts,
    sights, landscapes, buildings,
    persons
    stand outside us in our perception,
    knowing nothing of themselves
    by themselves.
    Nor do they express judgments.
    What is it then that does
    judge about them
    inside ourselves?
    The ruling faculty of Reason,
    the dubious gift of
    intellect and conceptual
    thinking.
    Beware!

16. Not in being passive
    but in being active
    lies the evil
    and the good
    of the rational social
    animal,
    a monkey body
    with a mischievous intellect.
    Virtue and vice also lie
    not in passivity,

but in being active,
so take care.

17. If a stone is thrown
up into the air
it is not evil that it
falls down,
nor indeed any good
that it was originally
thrown up.[29]
So be it.

18. Look closely into men's leading
principles
and you will detect what
their judges are afraid of,
and what kind of judges
they are themselves.

19. Everything changes all the time
and you, too, are in
continuous mutation,
preservation,
and destruction.
So is our home, of which we

---

[29] This verse is similar to viii. 20

BOOK IX. WISDOM

are a miserly tenant,
in the great universal mansion.

21. Express yourself,
bring your talents into
the world,
interact, harmonize
with "what is,"
do not conceal your
inner light
under a burden of consideration
I beg you.
But, termination of activity,
the end of action,
movement, and opinion
is not an evil
as if it is their death,
which is also not evil.
My father had a fond
relationship with me;
it made him happy,
now he is gone
where is the relationship?
Only in memory,
not in fact actually.
The Universe is your

friend,
embrace it!
Your folly is you feel separate,
but it brought you into being
and wishes to return you to
your Source,
so come home.
You've wandered enough in
the fields of alienation.
Marcus is in you
and you are in Marcus,
Marcus says "accept what is."
Wholeheartedly.

23. As you are a part of
    society
    let your acts be
    a contribution
    to that community's well-being.

25. Look into the quality of form
    in objects,
    detach it from its material
    and then contemplate,
    see how long it is destined
    to endure.

29. The universal force is like
a winter tempest,
it drives all along with it.
How worthless are all those
poor fools
engaged in politics,
who imagine they are playing
the part
of philosophers?
All deceptive drivellers,
driven by vanity.
So study well, do not expect
Utopia to arrive tomorrow,
but be happy if the smallest
thing goes well.
Regard such an event as
no small matter.
For who can change men
and women's principles?
And without a change of
principles
what remains but the slavery
of men who reluctantly obey?
Simple and modest is the
work of philosophy,
draw me not to insolence and pride.

30. Look down as if from above
    on the countless crowds of men
    and women
    and their innumerable solemnities,
    and their varied voyages in
    both storms and calms,
    and the differences amongst
    those who are born,
    live together,
    and die.
    Then reflect on the life
    lived by others
    in ancient days
    and the life of those who
    will live in the future.
    Also the life lived now
    by barbaric nations,
    and how many are unaware
    of your name,
    and how many will soon
    forget even that,
    and how now those who praise you
    will soon blame you.
    And that fame after
    death is valueless,
    as is reputation and riches.

BOOK IX. WISDOM

32. You can remove
out of the way
many useless things
which disturb you,
as these lie entirely
in your opinion
and you will gain great
space
by comprehending the whole
Universe in your mind,
by contemplating the eternity
of time
and noticing the rapid change
of each object
from its birth to dissolution.

35. Loss is nothing else
but change.
The universal Nature loves change,
and in obedience to her
all things are done well.
And from eternity have been done that way.
And will be so ad infinitum.
What then do you say?
That all things have been
and always will be largely suffering,
and that no power has been found

with even the Gods.
To correct this situation
the world has been so condemned
to be bound.[30]
Unless the self-referencing ego
is negated.

36. Matter, which is the
    basis of everything
    is fundamentally
    perishing.
    Water, dust, filth,
    marble, rocks, gold, silver,
    sediment, clothes, hair,
    purple dye, blood, and so on.
    Even our breath is of the
    same nature,
    changing from this to that.

37. Enough of this wretched life,
    murmuring, muttering,
    and apish tricks.
    Why are you upset?
    What's new in all this?

---

[30] This is the same view formed by Arthur Schopenhauer writing in the early nineteenth century, and before him the Buddha.

What disturbs you?
Is it the form of the thing?
Examine it.
Or is it the material itself?
Besides these everything
dissolves into no thing or
nothing.
It's the same whether
we look at these over
one hundred years.
Or three,
believe me.

39. Either all things proceed
from the intelligent Source
and come together in
one whole,
and parts must not find
fault with the whole,
or there are only random
atoms,
and nothing else but
mixtures and dispersions.
Why worry about this?
Say to the ruling faculty
of Reason,

Are you dead?
Are you corrupted?
Are you playing the hypocrite?
Have you become a beast?
Do you guzzle and wallow with
the rest of them?

40. Either the Gods have power
or no power.
If they have no power
why do you pray in a crisis?
But better to pray for
them to give you the power
of not fearing any of the
things which you now fear,
or not desiring any of the
things you desire,
or not being pained at all.
Begin to pray like this.
You will see
one man prays
"How shall I be able to
lie with that man or woman?"
Another prays
"How shall I be released
from that man or woman?"

BOOK IX. WISDOM

Another prays
"Please protect my little
son or daughter."
Well try and turn your
prayers to end fear and
watch what happens.

41. Epicurus said,[31] "In my illness,
my conversation was not
about my bodily suffering,
but on the nature of things.
My life went on well
and happily."
Do then the same in
sickness or health.
Never desert philosophy,
in any event which
may happen,
nor waste time in idle chatter
with ignoramuses,
but be intent on what
you are doing now
excellently.

[31] The philosopher who promoted the hedonist doctrine "Eat, drink and be merry for tomorrow we die."

42. When you are upset
    with anyone's shameless
    conduct
    towards you or others,
    ask yourself
    is it possible or not that
    this shameless man or woman
    should not be in the world?
    It is clearly possible,
    so do not require what is
    impossible then.
    This shameless man or woman
    must of necessity
    be in the world.
    This is true of the
    knave,
    rascal,
    faithless person,
    criminal,
    brute,
    and all wrongdoers.
    Once you see their necessity
    as part of the divine drama
    you will be better disposed
    toward them mentally.
    Virtue has given us the
    antidote against such people,

BOOK IX. WISDOM

for example, mildness,
or some other power.
You can always try to correct
the man or woman who
has gone astray.
Any evil done to you is
only in the mind.
When you do anything
benevolent, with goodwill,
compassionately,
for the common good
you have acted conformably
to what is right
and that is your reward,
Happiness!

BOOK X. PHILOSOPHY

1. Will you then, my soul,
   never be good and simple
   innocent, naked, honest,
   and even more noticeable
   than the vile body
   which envelops you?
   Will you never enjoy
   a contented
   disposition, calm and
   serene as a mountain lake?
   Will you ever be full,
   without a want, need,
   or desire, other than that which
   presents itself,
   never seeking endless pleasure,
   or stately villas,
   amenable people, only?
   Be satisfied with all that which
   presents itself
   to your consciousness;
   it comes from the Source of all being
   and what pleases that Source
   for inscrutable reasons of her
   own.
   So be at home and one with
   the Divine.
   Watch,

BOOK X. PHILOSOPHY

take notice,
my dear friends,
as to what thy true Nature
requires,
insofar as you are ruled by
Mother Nature.
There is no free will empirically,
only metaphysically![32]
So solve that mystery.
Your ego has to be dissolved
before you will understand
and you can only pray for that
to happen, I assure you.
All your efforts are God ordained,
but only to teach you,
ultimately you are governed
by them alone.
So surrender – or Self inquire
if you have time and effort,
energy on your hands,
and the power;
I love you all,
so do it!

[32] 'Mind and body are under the law of destiny. The soul is free in the attitude it takes
either to negate or affirm "what is." Phenomenal egolessness leads to numinous freedom
when the screen of appearances is pierced or unveiled.

Accept it!
Use these guidelines
and trouble yourself about
nothing else.

6. Whether our Universe is
    a mere concourse of atoms,
    or a great system of Nature,
    let this first be clearly
    understood,
    I am part of the whole,
    governed by Nature
    and intimately related
    to those parts similar to myself.
    So remembering this I shall
    not be discontented
    with anything given to me
    by the Whole.
    This leads to the conclusion
    that I shall do nothing harmful,
    antisocial,
    but rather work for the common
    good.
    This will make life to flow
    happily
    and my fellow citizens
    more contented

BOOK X. PHILOSOPHY

than they otherwise
might have been.

8. When you have assumed
these names
for yourself,
good,
modest,
true,
rational,
equitable,
magnanimous,
take care not to lose them.
To be rational means you
use
a discriminating attention to
every fact which comes your way
and freedom from negligence.
Equanimity is the voluntary
wholehearted acceptance of
whatever happens.
Magnanimity is the
elevation of your intelligence
above the slavery to pleasurable
or painful sensations of the flesh,
and above that bitch goddess fame
or fear of death's ghostly specter.

To lose these virtues and then
be reviled by your fellows
is the character of a stupid fool,
no better than a wounded beast
covered in bloody gore, clawed, and bitten.
Live as if thou dwelled in the
Islands of Happiness.[33]
If you do lose your virtues
then retire into some nook or cranny
where you can maintain
some vestige of them
not passionately,
but simply,
with freedom and modesty.
Never wish to be flattered,
remember the Gods, your mentors;
recall that which does
the work of a fig tree
is the power inherent in the
fig tree.
The fig tree does not worry
about how to produce figs,
as a dog is dog-life,
and a bee is a bee-life,
so to be an enlightened

---

[33] The Fortunate Insulae or Happy Isles are found in Greek, Roman, and Celtic folklore.

BOOK X. PHILOSOPHY

man, trust
that power which knows the
way,
and that does not mean
thinking overmuch about it.

12. What use is deadly
suspicious fear?
See clearly and take
the best advice instead.
He who follows reason
is both calm and active
as well as being cheerful
and Self collected.

13. Ask yourself on
arising from sleep
whether it will make
any essential difference to you
if another person does
what is just and right?
It will make no difference.
Remember, those who assume
pompous airs
in bestowing praise or blame,
often steal reputations by

the abuse or flattery
of those who simply choose
fidelity,
modesty,
truth,
law,
happiness.

15. There is only a little
life left for you,
so live as if you were
on a mountain peak.
For it matters little
where a man lives.
If he lives everywhere,
and sees the world as a
social community.
Let men see
and know a real man
who lives according
to his true nature.
If they cannot stand
his example
let them kill him
for it is better to be dead
than live
with such ignorant villains.

BOOK X. PHILOSOPHY

16. Stop talking about the
kind of man or woman
a good one should be,
but just simply be one.

19. Think what men are
when they are
eating,
sleeping,
procreating,
excreting,
imperious,
arrogant,
angry,
scolding from on high.
Consider a short time ago
to what they were enslaved
and for what?
Think in a short time
what condition they
shall be in?

21. The earth loves the rainfall,
the majestic sky is in love[34]
but the Universe loves to

[34] Euripides, Frag. 890. Shelley paraphrased this in his poem "Love's Philosophy."

make whatever is about to be.
So I love as the Universe loves.

25. He who flies from his master
    is a "runaway"
    but the divine law
    is our master
    and he who resists the
    divine will
    is attempting to be
    a "runaway" from "what is."
    Such is he who is aggrieved,
    angry,
    afraid,
    worried,
    morose,
    because something should have been
    or is or may be,
    which he does not like.
    Such is the character of
    the "runaway" slave.

26. A man sheds his seed
    in a womb
    and leaves.
    Another cause takes over,
    works,

BOOK X. PHILOSOPHY

and a child is born.
What a miracle
from such material!
Similarly the child eats,
another cause takes over,
creates his perception and motion,
fine health and strength.
How miraculous!
Notice how that which is created
is made in a secret hidden way.
And see its power
like the power of gravity,[35]
not with the eyes
but just as clearly.

27. Constantly ponder how all
things such as they are now,
were in times past.
And reflect that they will be
the same again,
and imagine entire dramas
and stages of the same pattern.
For all the plays of
the past

---

[35] Marcus refers to the power that carries things downwards and upwards. The later concept of gravity was an insight of Sir Isaac Newton.

were such dramas as we see
now, only with fresh actors.[36]

28. Imagine
each man or woman who is
grieved,
and discontented
is like a pig or sow which
is due for sacrifice
and kicks and screams,
before his throat is slit,
and he is slowly bled to death.
Such is our physical animality,
but not the soul.
Like this pig or sow
is he or she who in their bed
bemoans his or her situation;
instead she or he must welcome
wholeheartedly
all that is,
including his objections
and the situation will be
miraculously reversed
because he or she is now
in harmony with the divine will.

[36] Arthur Schopenhauer's view of history was very similar to this, unlike Georg Hegel who
saw it as a progression.

BOOK X. PHILOSOPHY

30. If you are outraged
    by another man or woman's
    fault,
    turn to yourself
    and see when
    you have [acted?] in the same way.
    For example, in being
    miserly with money,
    then spending too much time
    thinking about it,
    then going on a spending binge,
    or wallowing in carnal pleasures,
    or trying to enhance your
    reputation
    in the eyes of others.
    In this way you will forget
    your anger,
    remembering that the man
    or woman
    who outraged you was compelled
    by necessity,
    he could act in no other way
    than the way he did,
    like you did too.
    If you can, remove the cause
    of his compulsion.

33. A man should
    consider as an enjoyment
    all which it is in his power
    to perform
    according to his nature,
    as a rational being.
    It is in his power everywhere.
    It is not given to a cylinder
    to move wherever it wishes
    not even to water,
    nor fire.
    But intelligence and reason
    are able to go through everything,
    and everywhere,
    that opposes them.

34. To that man or woman,
    permeated and penetrated
    by pure principles,
    even the briefest perception
    is enough to see.
    "Leaves, sometimes the wind
    scatters,
    so with the race of men."[37]
    For all things, as the poet says

---

[37] Homer, Iliad VI 146.

BOOK X. PHILOSOPHY

"Are born in the season of
Spring, then the wind casts
them down,
then the forest grows other
leaves in their places,
in Autumn they turn gold
and are brought down
by the wild west wind."

35. The healthy eye ought to
see all visible things
and not make preferences
to wish for more green, and less red,
and so on.
This is the condition of
a diseased eye.
The healthy hearing and
smelling
should be ready to perceive
all that can be heard and
smelled.
The healthy stomach should
be with respect to food
as the mill respects all which
it is formed to grind.

Above all, the healthy understanding
welcomes everything which
comes into purview.
But that which moans,
"let all my children live
happily, let all men praise
my acts"
is like the eye which seeks only
for greenery,
or teeth which will only
enjoy soft invalid foods.

36. There is nobody so
lucky as when he is dying,
there shall be some
who are secretly pleased.
Suppose he or she was
good and wise,
but keeping your own
character,
being friendly and kind,
die quietly;
so the soul easily and gently
leaves the body,
for an unknown adventure
in the hands of the Gods.

BOOK X. PHILOSOPHY

38. Remember well
  that which pulls the
  strings[38]
  is the ruler hidden within.
  This is the power of necessity,
  this is life,
  this is puppet man and woman.
  In reflection never include
  the vessel
  surrounding one
  and the instruments attached to it,
  there is no more use in
  these parts
  without the cause which
  moves and checks them,
  than in the weaver's shuttle,
  the writer's pen,
  the driver's whip,
  the surgeon's scalpel.

[38] The same metaphor is coincidentally used in the end of the Bhagavad Gita, Ch. 18.

BOOK XI. TRUTHS

1. These are the properties
   of the rational Soul:
   it sees itself,
   analyzes itself,
   makes itself such as it
   chooses.
   The fruit which it
   bears, itself enjoys.
   It obtains its own end,
   not as an actor in a dance or drama,
   but fully and completely
   so it can say
   I own that which is my
   own.
   It traverses the whole
   Universe,
   surveys its form,
   extends into infinity,
   comprehends the renewal
   of all things.
   He who has reached the
   mature age
   of forty years
   will understand this
   unanimity.
   This too is a property
   of the rational Soul,

love of one's neighbor,
truth,
modesty.
Right Reason is the same as the
Reason of Justice.

You will not set much value
on pleasing songs, dancing,
or watching fights between thugs
and wrestlers.
If you split the melody of
song into its different notes
and listen to the effect of each on you,
and study your emotions in
dancing and watching fights,
then you will see how
much more valuable is virtue
and the virtuous act,
than these side shows.

6. Tragedies are performed
   on stage
   to remind men and women
   of what can happen in life,
   and if you are delighted by
   the drama
   you will not be troubled

by what takes place
on the stage of life.
Much has been well said
by playwrights
such as
me and my children, if
the Gods neglect them,
this has good reasons too.[39]
We must not regret and fret
at that which happens.[40]
Life's harvest is reaped like
the wheat's fruitful ear.[41]
After tragedy came comedy,
which reminded men to beware
The light comedy which followed
sank down into mere mimicry
and artificiality,
The whole plan of such banal
poetry.
To what end does it seek?

7. How obvious that there is not
    any condition of life
    so well suited for philosophy

---

[39] From Aristophones, Acharnenses.
[40] From Euripedes, Bellerephon.
[41] From Euripedes, Hypsipyle.

as that in which you
happen to be now!

8. A branch cut off
   from a main branch
   is necessarily cut off
   from the whole tree too.
   So is a man separated
   from another man
   cut off from the social
   community.
   As to a branch, an axe-man
   severs it off,
   but by his own deed a man
   cuts himself off from his neighbor
   when he hates him.
   Thus he cuts himself off from
   our social system.
   But it is in our power to
   grow again to that which is
   near and dear to us
   and again unite with
   the part which makes up the whole.

10. There is no nature which is
    inferior to art,
    for the arts imitate the

nature of things.
So, that nature which is
the most perfect and comprehensive
of all natures
cannot fall short of the
skill of art.
Now all arts do the
inferior things
for the sake of the superior,
so does the universal nature also.
This is the origin of Justice
and in Justice the other virtues
have their foundation.
Justice will not be observed,
if we only care for trivial matters
or are easily deceived, careless
and changeable like the chameleon.

15. Unsound and insincere
is he who says
"I am going to deal with you
in a fair way."
What are you doing?
There is no need to give this
notice.
It will soon show itself by your
deeds.

Your voice ought to be plainly
written on your forehead;
you cannot make a crooked
stick straight.
Such as a man's character is,
he shows in his eyes,
as lovers read all
in each other's eyes.
The honest and good
are like the man who gives
forth strength
so that whoever comes near him
senses his strength.
But the affectation of fairness
is like the crooked stick.
Nothing is more disgraceful than
a false wolfish friendship.
Avoid this above all and
be good, just, and simple.
Show all these virtues in your gaze
and there is no mistake.

18. If any have offended you
think first, what is my
relationship to men and women
when we are made for another?
In my case I was destined

to be set over them
as a ram over a flock of sheep,
or a bull over a herd of cattle.
Reason tells me that if all things
are not atoms alone
it is nature which orders
events.
Thus the inferior exists for
the sake of the superior
and these for the sake of one
another.
Secondly, visualize what
kind of men they really are
at the dining table,
sleeping in bed,
easing themselves,
and in their houses.
Under what compulsions
and opinions are they?
As to their deeds, take
note of their pride.
Thirdly, if men and women
act rightly
we are pleased
but if they do wrong,
it is obvious they do so
involuntarily

BOOK XI. TRUTHS

and in ignorance.
Fourthly, reflect on one's own
Wrongdoing;
you too are a man or woman,
and even if you do abstain
from certain faults,
still you have the desire
to do them
either through cowardice,
concern about one's reputation,
or other mean motives.
Fifth, reflect that you do not
really know
whether men and women are
doing wrong or not.
Most deeds are done through force
of circumstance
so a man or woman must know
a great deal
to enable him to pass a correct judgment
on another's acts.
Sixth, remember when you are
worried or upset,
that your life is only for a
moment,
like the mayfly in Summer,

and after a while we are all
laid out dead,
ready for the washers.
Seventh, it is not really the deeds
of others
that worry us,
it is our own opinions
which disturb
our thoughts and feelings.
Take away these opinions
and the disturbance has gone!
Eighth, reflect how much more
pain is brought about
by our anger and vexation
than the acts themselves.
Ninth, genuine goodwill
is invincible and not a sham.
What can the most violent do
if you continue to be benevolent
towards him or her?
If the chance arises,
gently advise him or her,
calmly correct his or her error,
saying "not so my child
we are made by the Gods
for something better,

BOOK XI. TRUTHS

I shall not be hurt by you
but you are hurting yourself
my child."
Then show him or her with gentle tact
and prove by the principles of reason
that this is the case;
even bees do not act as he or she does,
nor any social animals.
This must not be done with
double meaning
or as a reproach
but affectionately, warmly,
without rancor,
and not as a lecture.
Remember these nine rules
as if they were a gift from the muses,
and begin at last to be a true
man or woman as long as you live.
But you must avoid flattering
as much as being annoyed,
both are antisocial and lead to harm.
Bring this truth to consciousness
in the excitement of anger,
remember, to be moved by passion
is unworthy,
mildness and gentleness are more
agreeable.

He who has these qualities
possesses strength, nerve, courage.
Not the man or woman
subject to fits of passion and complaint.
In the same degree as a man or woman's
mind is free of passion,
so is it nearer to strength.
The sense of pain, as is anger,
are weaknesses,
yielding to either, one is wounded.
Now here is a tenth gift from
the muses,
to expect wicked men and women
not to do wrong is madness,
and to allow them to behave
in this way
is irrational and tyrannical.

19. There are four principal
    perversions
    of your superior rational
    faculty
    against which constantly guard.
    Once one has spotted them
    you must wipe them out ruthlessly.
    One, as unnecessary,
    two as antisocial unworthy thoughts,

three, as not genuinely spoken
from the heart.
Four, as that of self-condemnation
or reproach
for that is admission of that the
divine part within you
is being overpowered and
yielding to the less honorable,
perishing body and
its gross pleasures.

20. Your airy part and fiery[42]
parts are mingled.
By nature they strive to ascend,
but in obedience to the universal
will, they are overpowered in
the mass of the gross body.
So the earthy and watery
parts,
although their tendency is heavy,
are still raised up, for them
unnaturally.
So the elemental in us obeys the
universal
and remains fixed in its place

[42]This verse was used as the preface to Part V of Thomas Hardy's masterpiece novel
Jude the Obscure.

until its dissolution.
It is strange that your
intelligence
should be discontented and
disobedient to its allotted place.
The movement towards injustice,
intemperance,
anger,
grief,
fear,
are deviations from nature.
So when the ruling rational
mind
is unhappy with what happens
it deserts its post.
It is made for respect and
reverence
towards the Divine Source of all being,
its own Source,
no less than for justice.
These qualities are understood
as affirming the way "things are"
and it comes before any
just deeds.

BOOK XI. TRUTHS

21. He who has not one and
the same aim in life
cannot remain one and
the same.
This aim should be
for the entire common social welfare.

22. Think about the country
mouse
and the town mouse.
The town mouse is in a
constant state of alarm and
fear.[43]
The country mouse is happy.

23. The great and wise
Socrates
nicknamed the opinions of
the mob
ghouls or bogies to
frighten little children.

25. Socrates excused himself to
Archelaus,
for not visiting him,

[43] This tale comes from Horace (Satires II.6).

at his Court,
because he refused to perish
by the worst of all ends,
to receive a favor
and then be unable to return it.

27. The Pythagorean philosophies
advised us every morning
to look at the heavens,
so we may be reminded of all
those planetary bodies
which always perform their work
faithfully, in a pure state
of nudity,
there is no veil over a star!

28. Reflect on the nobility
of Socrates:
when his shrewish wife
Xanthippe
hid his cloak and went out
he dressed himself in a
goat skin.
And how Socrates admonished
his friends
who were then ashamed to be

with him
when he was dressed like this.

29. Neither in writing
    nor in reading
    can you lay down rules
    for others
    before you have learned to
    obey rules yourself,
    this applies to the whole
    of life.

33. To look for a fig
    in Winter
    is the work of a mad man,
    like the idiot who searches
    for his child
    when he no longer has one.[44]

34. When a man kisses
    his child,
    said Epictetus,
    he should whistle to himself
    "Tomorrow perhaps you will
    die."

[44] This is from Epictetus III.24.

Are these words of bad omen?
"No word is a word of
bad omen"
said Epictetus
"which expresses any
work of nature, it is no different
than speaking about ears of
corn soon to be reaped."

35. The unripe grape,
the ripe bunch,
the dried grape,
all are changes
not into nothing
but into something
which is not yet there.[45]

37. Epictetus also said that
a man or woman
must discover the art of
saying "yes"
and watch that his movements
conform with circumstances
consistent with social interests
regarding the value of the aim.

[45] Also from Epictetus III.24.

BOOK XI. TRUTHS

He wanted men to refrain
from excessive sexual desire
and not to show aversion to
anything out of our control.

38. Finally, Socrates asked
    "what do you want?
    Souls of rational men or
    Irrational beasts?"
    Souls of rational men:
    what kind of rational men,
    sound or unsound?
    If sound, why do you not
    seek for them,
    because we know who they are;
    why do you quarrel and argue?

BOOK XII. CONCLUSIONS

1. Everything at which you
   wish to reach
   by a roundabout route
   you can have now,
   directly,
   if you don't refuse
   them yourself.
   This means forget the past,
   leave the future to
   divine providence,
   while directing the present.
   Respect religious values
   and justice,
   so you may be content
   with your place
   given to you by Nature,
   who designed it specially for you,
   and you for her.
   Just so as you may always
   speak truth freely
   without disguise,
   be law abiding
   and value the worth of
   every man and woman.
   Never let anybody's wickedness
   hinder you,
   nor their opinions

BOOK XII. CONCLUSIONS

nor their speech.
Do not allow any sensation
of the flesh to weaken you.
Whatever the time may be
near death
forget all else,
respect your ruling rational mind,
and the divinity within your
heart.
Then you will not fear because
death is inevitable for all.
Fear is a result of never having started
living according to Nature.
This will make you worthy of the Universe,
which created you.
You will then cease to be
a stranger in your homeland,
and to wonder at daily events
as if they were unexpected,
and to be dependent on
this or that.

The divine sees the minds
of all mankind
stripped of material skin, pith,
pips, rind, and impurities,
with His intellectual perception

alone.
He touches the intelligence
which has emanated from
Himself
into these bodies.
And if you also do this,
you will rid yourself of
many troubling thoughts.
For he who disregards
the weak flesh
which clothes him or her
will surely not worry
by seeking after fashions,
houses, fame,
and similar ostentations.

You are composed of three
elements,
body,
life breath,
intelligence.
Body and life breath are
yours
insofar as it is your duty
to look after them,
but the third, alone, is properly
yours.

BOOK XII. CONCLUSIONS

So if you separate from your
"understanding"
whatever others say or do,
and whatever you have said or done,
and any future troubles,
that you imagine may happen,
then whatever in the body or the life breath,
is attached to you independently of
your will,
and whatever circumstances whirl
around you,
so your intellectual power
free from fate,
can live purely,
acting justly,
accepting "what is"
wholeheartedly,
speaking the truth
without fear.
So if you will separate
from your rational ruling mind
the things attached to it
by sense impressions,
and what may come in time,
and what happened in the past,

you will be like the sphere of
Empedocles,[46]
"All embracing, and at joyous rest."
Then if you strive to live
only what is truly thy life,
that is in the present moment,
you will be able to live
the rest of your life
free from mental stress,
nobly,
like an Emperor,
obedient to that God within
you.

I have often pondered
how is it every man and
woman
loves their own Self more than
all the rest of mankind,
yet sets less value on his
own opinion of himself
than on the opinion of others?
If then a God or a Sage
presents himself to a man
and tells him to think of

[46] A Stoic philosopher.

BOOK XII. CONCLUSIONS

nothing at all,
which he should not express,
even if he could conceive it,
he would not endure it
even for a day.

How can it possibly be
that the Gods, having ordered
all things well and benevolently,
have overlooked this alone,
that some very good men and
women, who communed with
the Deity
intimately,
when once they left the body
should be transmigrated
and never return in a recognizable
form?
If it was good to be otherwise
I am sure the Gods would have
ordained it.
In this inquiry we are disputing
with God's will
and this is not a worthy endeavor.

Practice even in activities
your despair of mastering.

Even the left hand, which
is generally less effective
than the right, holds the bridle
more vigorously when on horseback,
as it has been exercised
in this well.

9. In the application of rational principles
    you must be as the boxer or wrestler,
    not as the gladiator.
    If the gladiator drops his
    sword he is killed,
    but the other always has
    his hands and only needs to use them,
    to defeat his foe.

11. Men and women have
    no power
    to do anything unless
    it is allowed by God's will.
    One must accept this law
    wholeheartedly.

12. With respect to all that
    which happens
    driven by Nature's law
    of necessity

BOOK XII. CONCLUSIONS

we ought to blame neither
the Gods
nor men, for they do nothing
wrong except involuntarily.
So we should blame nobody,
although we might disapprove.

13. How absurd it is
    to be surprised at anything
    which happens in life.

15. Does the lamplight shine
    without losing its splendor
    until it is switched off?
    Shall the truth,
    Justice, and moderation
    in you, be switched off
    before thy death?

16. Reflect, he or she who would
    not have a bad person do wrong,
    is like the man who would
    not have fig trees to produce fig juice,
    or babies cry and horses neigh.
    Once you have seen this and are
    still irritable,

then cure this disposition by
rational argument.

18. In all perception
always see what object
produces for you its appearance.
Then resolve it by dividing it
into its form,
its matter,
its purpose,
its duration.

19. This may lead you to
an apperception of
the "thing in itself."

25. Throw away opinions,
toss them in the rubbish heap,
you are now saved.
What stops you from
getting rid of them?

27. Reflect on those who
have complained bitterly,
think where are they now?
Smoke, ash, and

BOOK XII. CONCLUSIONS

a sad story.
Think too of the eager hunt
for anything connected
with pride, pomp, and vanity,
and how worthless they are.
Be philosophical instead.

28. To those who mock,
    "Have you actually seen
    the Gods?
    How do you know they
    really exist?"
    I answer, neither have I seen
    my own soul
    yet I honor it
    and with the Gods
    I constantly experience their
    powers
    and this is sufficient.

29. Enjoy life,
    join one good event
    to another
    so as not to leave even
    the smallest gap in between.

36. My dearest men and women,
    you are citizens
    in this great State of
    the World.
    What difference does
    it make to you
    whether you live for five years
    or a hundred?
    For under its laws
    equal treatment is
    dealt to all
    by Grace.
    Even He that sacks you
    in the end,
    is Gracious too.

So be it

Marcus Aurelius Antoninus
Emperor of Rome

AN ESSAY ON
MARCUS AURELIUS BY
MATTHEW ARNOLD

APPENDIX 1.

Matthew Arnold (1822-1888), English critic and poet, was the son of Thomas Arnold (1795-1842), the clergyman who became headmaster of Rugby and made it one of England's most renowned public schools. Young Arnold began his literary career as a poet, publishing *The Strayed Reveler and Other Poems* (1849); *Empedocles on Etna and Other Poems* (1852); *Poems* (1853); *Poems, Second Series* (1855); *Merope,* a dramatic poem (1858); and *New Poems* (1867). His poetry tends to be elegiac and brooding, and at its best is among the finest expressions of the plight of the sensitive Victorian caught between "two worlds, one dead, the other powerless to be born." His most famous poems are "The Scholar-Gipsy"; based on the legend of an Oxford student who, in poverty, joined a band of gypsies; "Stanzas from the Grande Chartreuse" (1855), in which the narrator, visiting a Carthusian monastery, mourns the loss of faith in the modern world; "Thyrsis" (1866), an elegy written on the death of Arnold's friend Arthur Hugh Clough, which Swinburne adjudged, after Milton's "Lycidas" and Shelley's "Adonais," the finest elegy in the English language; and "Dover Beach," perhaps his best known poem, which uses the image of the sea as a metaphor for the Sea of Faith, ebbing away from the naked shores of the world.

In 1857 Arnold was elected to the professorship of poetry at Oxford. During the ten years that he held this position, he delivered many of the lectures that were to become part of his essays on criticism. The best known collections of these are *On Translating Homer* (1861), *Essays in Criticism* (1st Series, 1865; 2nd series, 1888), *Culture and Anarchy*, and *Literature and Dogma* (1873). Seeing literature as both shaper and sustainer of the highest elements of culture, he urged that the great mass of the public – the "philistine" middle class – be educated to improve to improve its response to literature (and culture). He argued for high standards of literary judgment, using the "lines and expressions of the great masters ... as a touchstone to other poetry." He believed that the English were too immersed in the spirit of "Hebraism," or strictness of conscience and rightness of conduct, and not sufficiently touched by the symmetry and spontaneity of "Hellenism," he saw religious fundamentalism as one expression of this Hebraism, and Arnold attempted to interpret the Bible as literature and show that, as in all great poetry, the poetry of the Bible contained the moral and spiritual truths that were the essence of religion. He saw the task of the critic as "a disinterested endeavor to learn and propagate the best that is known and thought in the world." He is of importance as a shaper of both English and American criticism, up to the time of T. S. Eliot.

MARCUS AURELIUS
BY MATTHEW ARNOLD[7]

Mr John Stuart Mill says, in his book on Liberty, that
'Christian morality is in great part merely a protest against
paganism; its ideal is negative rather than positive, passive
rather than active'. He says that, in certain most important
respects, 'it falls far below the best morality of the
ancients'. The object of systems of morality is to take
possession of human life, to save it from being abandoned
to passion or allowed to drift at hazard, to give it happiness
by establishing it in the practice of virtue; and this object
they seek to attain by prescribing to human life fixed
principles of action, fixed rules of conduct. In its
uninspired as well as in its inspired moments, in its days of
languor and gloom as well as in its days of sunshine and
energy, human life has thus always a clue to follow, and
may always be making way towards its goal. Christian
morality has not failed to supply to human life aids of this
sort. It has supplied them far more abundantly than most
of its critics imagine. The most exquisite document, after
those of the New Testament, of all that the Christian spirit

[7] I have slightly edited and abridged this essay – mainly the comparison between the Long
and Collier translations.

has ever inspired – the Imitation by Thomas a Kempis, by no means contains the whole of Christian morality; nay, the disparagers of this morality would think themselves sure of triumphing if one agreed to look for it in the Imitation only. But even the Imitation is full of passages like these, *'Every day we ought to renew our purpose, saying to ourselves: This day let us make a sound beginning, for what we have hitherto done is naught'*, *'Our improvement is in proportion to our purpose'*, *We hardly ever manage to get completely rid even of one fault, and do not set our hearts on daily improvement'*, *'Always place a definite purpose before thee'*, *'Get the habit of mastering thine inclination'*. These are moral precepts, and moral precepts of the best kind. As rules to hold possession of our conduct, and to keep us in the right course through outward troubles and inward perplexity, they are equal to the best ever furnished by the great masters of morals – Epictetus or Marcus Aurelius.

But moral rules, apprehended as ideas first, and then rigorously followed as laws, are, and must be, for the Sage only. The mass of mankind have neither force of intellect enough to apprehend them clearly as ideas, nor force of character enough to follow them strictly as laws. The mass of mankind can be carried along a course full of hardship for the natural man, can be borne over the thousand impediments of the narrow way, only by the tide of a joyful and bounding emotion. It is impossible to rise from reading Epictetus or Marcus Aurelius without a sense of constraint and melancholy, without feeling that the burden laid upon man is well-nigh greater than he can bear. Honour to the Sages who have felt this, and yet have borne it! Yet, even for the Sage, this sense of labour and sorrow in his march towards the goal constitutes a relative inferiority; the noblest souls of whatever creed, the pagan Empedocles as well as the Christian Paul, have insisted on the necessity of an inspiration, a living emotion, to make moral action perfect; an obscure indication of this necessity is the one drop of truth in the ocean of verbiage with which the controversy on justification by faith has flooded the world. But, for the ordinary man, this sense of labour and sorrow constitutes an absolute disqualification; it paralyses him; under the weight of it, he cannot make way towards the goal at all. The paramount virtue of religion is, that it has *"lit up"* morality; that it has supplied the emotion and inspiration needful for carrying the Sage along the narrow way perfectly, for carrying the ordinary man along it at all. Even the religions with most dross in them have had something of this virtue; but the Christian religion manifests it with unexampled splendour. 'Lead me, Zeus and providence', says the prayer of Epictetus, 'whithersoever I am appointed to go; I will follow without wavering; even though I turn coward and shrink, I shall have to follow all the same'. The fortitude of that is for the strong, for the few; even for them, the spiritual atmosphere with which it surrounds them is bleak and grey. But 'let thy loving spirit lead me forth into the land of righteousness', 'The Lord shall be unto thee an everlasting light, and thy God they glory', 'Unto you that fear My Name shall the Son of Righteousness arise with healing in his wings' says the Old Testament; 'Born, not of blood, nor of the will of the flesh, nor of the will of man, but of God', 'Except a man be born again, he cannot see the kingdom of God', 'Whatsoever is born of God, overcometh the world' says the New. The ray of sunshine is there, the glow of a divine warmth: the austerity of the Sage melts away under it, the paralysis of the weak is healed; he who is vivified by it renews his strength; 'all things are possible to Him'; 'he is a new creature'.

Epictetus says 'Every matter has two handles, one of which will bear taking hold of, the other not. If thy brother sin against thee, lay not hold of the matter by this, that he sins against thee; for by this handle the matter will not bear taking hold of. But rather lay hold of it by this, that he is thy brother, thy born mate; and thou wilt take hold of it by what will bear handling'. Jesus, asked whether a man is bound to forgive his brother as often as seven times, answers 'I say not unto thee, until seven times, but until seventy times seven'. Epictetus here suggests to the reason grounds for forgiveness of injuries which Jesus does not; but it is vain to say that Epictetus is on that account a better moralist than Jesus, if the warmth, the emotion, of Jesus's answer fires his hearer to the practice of forgiveness of injuries, while the thought in Epictetus's leaves him cold. So with Christian morality in general; its distinction is not that it propounds the maxim 'Thou shalt love God and thy neighbour', with more development, close reasoning, truer sincerity, than other moral systems; it is that it propounds this maxim with an inspiration which wonderfully catches the hearer and makes him act upon it. It is because Mr Mill has attained to the perception of truths of this nature, that he is – instead of being, like the school from which he proceeds, doomed to sterility – a writer of distinguished mark and influence, a writer deserving all attention and respect; it is (I must be pardoned for saying) because he is not sufficiently leavened with them, that he falls just short of being a great writer.

That which gives to the moral writings of the Emperor Marcus Aurelius their peculiar character and charm, is their being suffused and softened by something of this very sentiment whence Christian morality draws its best power. Mr Long has recently published in a convenient form a translation of these writings, and has thus enabled English readers to judge Marcus Aurelius for themselves; he has rendered his countrymen a real service by so doing. Mr Long's reputation as a scholar is a sufficient guarantee of the general fidelity and accuracy of his translation; on these matters, besides, I am hardly entitled to speak, and my praise is of no value. But that for which I and the rest of the unlearned may venture to praise Mr Long is this; that he treats Marcus Aurelius's writings, as he treats all the other remains of Greek and Roman antiquity which he touches, not as a dead and dry matter of learning, but as documents with a side of modern applicability and living interest, and valuable mainly so far as this side in them can be made clear, that as in his notes on Plutarch's Roman *Lives* he deals with the modern epoch of Caesar and Cicero, not as food for schoolboys, but as food for men, and men engaged in the current of contemporary life and action, so in his remarks and essays on Marcus Aurelius, he treats this truly modern striver and thinker not as a 'Classical Dictionary' hero, but as a present source from which to draw 'example of life, and instruction of manners'. Why may not a son of Dr Arnold say, what might naturally here be said by any other critic, that in this lively and fruitful way of considering the men and affairs of ancient Greece and Rome, Mr Long resembles Dr Arnold?

One must express unfeigned gratitude to Mr Long for his excellent and substantial reproduction in English of an invaluable work. In general the substantiality, soundness, and precision of his rendering are (I cannot but think) as conspicuous as the living spirit with which he treats antiquity; and these qualities are particularly desirable in the translator of a work like Marcus Aurelius's, of which the language is often corrupt, almost always hard and obscure. Anyone who wants to appreciate Mr Long's merits as a translator may read, in the original and in Mr Long's translation, the seventh chapter of the tenth book; he will see how, through all the dubiousness and involved manner of the Greek, Mr Long has firmly seized upon the clear thought which is certainly at the bottom of that troubled wording and, in distinctly rendering this thought, has at the same time thrown round its expression a characteristic shade of painfulness and difficulty which just suits it. And Marcus Aurelius's book is one which, when it is rendered so accurately as Mr Long renders it, even those who know Greek tolerably well may choose to read rather in the translation than in the original. For not only are the contents here incomparably more valuable than the external form, but this form, this Greek of a Roman, is not one of those styles which have a physiognomy, which are an essential part of their author, which stamp an indelible impression of him on the reader's mind. An old Lyons commentator finds, indeed, in Marcus Aurelius's Greek, something characteristic, something specially firm and imperial; but I think and ordinary mortal will hardly find this;

he will find crabbed Greek, without any charm of distinct physiognomy. The Greek of Thucydides and Plato has this charm, and he who reads them in a translation, however accurate, loses it, and loses much in losing it; but the Greek of Marcus Aurelius, like the Greek of the New Testament, is wanting in it. If one could be assured that the English Testament were made perfectly accurate, one might be perfectly content never to open a Greek Testament again; and, Mr Long's version of Marcus Aurelius being what it is, and Englishman who reads to live, and does not live to read, may henceforth let the Greek original repose upon itself.

The man whose thoughts Mr Long has thus faithfully reproduced, is perhaps the most beautiful figure in history. He is one of those consoling and hope-inspiring marks, which stand for ever to remind our weak and easily discouraged race how high human goodness and perseverance have once been carried, and may be carried again. The interest of mankind is peculiarly attracted by examples of signal goodness in high places; for that testimony to the worth of goodness is the most striking which is borne by those to whom all means of pleasure and self-indulgence lay open, by those who had at their command the kingdoms of the world and the glory of them. Marcus Aurelius was the ruler of the grandest of empires; and he was one of the best of men. Besides him, history presents one or two other sovereigns eminent for their goodness, such as Saint Louis or King Alfred. But Marcus Aurelius has, for us moderns, this great superiority in interest over Saint Louis or Alfred, that he lived and acted in a state of society modern by its essential characteristics, in an epoch akin to our own, in a brilliant centre of civilisation. Trajan talks of 'our enlightened age' just as glibly as *The Times* talks of it. Marcus Aurelius thus becomes for us a man like ourselves, a man in all things tempted as we are. Saint Louis inhabits an atmosphere of mediæval catholicism, which the man of the nineteenth century may admire, indeed, may even passionately wish to inhabit, but which, strive as he will, he cannot really inhabit; Alfred belongs to a state of society (I say it with all deference to *The Saturday Review* critic who keeps such jealous watch over the honour of our Saxon ancestors) half barbarous. Neither Alfred or Saint Louis can be morally and intellectually as near to us as Marcus Aurelius.

The record of the outward life of this admirable man has in it little of striking incident. He was born at Rome on the 26th April, in the year 121 of the Christian era. He was nephew and son-in-law to his predecessor on the throne, Antoninus Pius. When Antoninus died, he was forty years old, but from the time of his earliest manhood he had assisted in administering public affairs. Then, after his uncle's death in 161 for nineteen years he reigned as emperor. The barbarians were pressing on the Roman frontier, and a great part of Marcus Aurelius's nineteen years of reign was passed in campaigning. His absences from Rome were numerous and long; we hear of him in Asia Minor, Syria, Egypt, Greece; but, above all, in the countries on the Danube, where the war with the barbarians was going on – in Austria, Moravia, Hungary. In these countries much of his *Journal* seems to have been written; parts of it are dated from them; and there, a few weeks before his fifty-ninth birthday, he fell sick and died.[8] The record of him on which his fame chiefly rests is the record of his inward life – his *Journal*, or *Commentaries*, or *Meditations*, or *Thoughts*, for by all these names has the work been called. Perhaps the most interesting of the record of his outward life is that which the first book of this work supplies, where he gives an account of his education, recites the names of those to whom he is indebted for it, and enumerates his obligations to each of them. It is a refreshing and consoling picture, a priceless treasure for those, who, sick of the 'wild and dreamlike trade of blood and guile', which seems to be nearly the whole that history has to offer to our view, seek eagerly for that substratum of right thinking and well doing which in all ages must

---

[8] He died on the 17th March, 180.

surely have somewhere existed, for without it the continued life of
humanity would have been impossible. 'From my mother I learnt piety
and beneficence, and the abstinence not only from evil deeds but even
from evil thoughts; and further, simplicity in my way of living, far
removed from the habits of the rich'. Let us remember that, the next
time we are reading the sixth satire of Juvenal. 'From my tutor I learnt'
(hear it, ye tutors of princes!) 'endurance of labour, and to want little,
and to work with my own hands, and not to meddle with other people's
affairs, and not to be ready to listen to slander'. The vices and foibles of
the Greek sophist or rhetorician – the *Græculus esuriens* – are in
everybody's mind; but he who reads Marcus Aurelius's account of his
Greek teachers and masters, will understand how it is that, in spite of the
vices and foibles of individual *Græculi*, the education of the human race
owes to Greece a debt which can never be overrated. The vague and
colourless praise of history leaves on the mind hardly any impression of
Antoninus Pius; it is only from the private memoranda of his nephew
that we learn what a disciplined, hard-working, gentle, wise, virtuous
man he was; a man who, perhaps, interests mankind less than his
immortal nephew only because he has left in writing no record of his
inner life. Of the outward life and circumstances of Marcus Aurelius,
beyond these notices which he has himself supplied, there are few of
much interest and importance. There is the fine anecdote of his speech
when he heard of the assassination of the revolted Avidius Cassius,
against whom he was marching; *he was sorry,* he said, *to be deprived of the
pleasure of pardoning him.* And there are one or two more anecdotes of
him which show the same spirit. But the great record for the outward
life of a man who has left such a record of his lofty inward aspirations as
that which Marcus Aurelius has left, is the clear consenting voice of all
his contemporaries – high and low, friend and enemy, pagan and
Christian – in praise of his sincerity, justice, and goodness. The world's
charity does not err on the side of excess, and here was a man
occupying the most conspicuous station in the world, and professing the

highest possible standard of conduct; yet the world was obliged to declare that he walked worthily of his profession. Long after his death, his bust was to be seen in the houses of private men through the wide Roman empire; it may be the vulgar part of human nature which busies itself with the semblance and doings of living sovereigns, it is its nobler part which busies itself with those of the dead; these busts of Marcus Aurelius, in the homes of Gaul, Britain, and Italy, bore witness, not to the inmates' frivolous curiosity about princes and palaces, but to their reverential memory of the passage of a great man upon the earth.

Two things, however, before one turns from the outward to the inward life of Marcus Aurelius, force themselves upon one's notice, and demand a word of comment; he persecuted the Christians, and he had for his son the vicious and brutal Commodus. The persecution at Lyons, in which Attalus and Pothinus suffered, the persecution at Smyrna in which Polycarp suffered, took place in his reign. Of his humanity, of his tolerance, of his horror of cruelty and violence, of his wish to refrain from severe measures against the Christians, of his anxiety to temper the severity of these measures when they appeared to him indispensable, there is no doubt; but, on the one hand, it is certain that the letter, attributed to him, directing that no Christian should be punished for being a Christian, is spurious; it is almost certain that his alleged answer to the authorities of Lyons, in which he directs that Christians persisting in their profession shall be dealt with according to law, is genuine. Mr Long seems inclined to try and throw doubt over the persecution at Lyons, by pointing out that the letter of the Lyons Christians relating it, alleges it to have been attended by miraculous and incredible incidents'. 'A man', he says, 'can only act consistently, by accepting all this letter or rejecting it all, and we cannot blame him for either'. But it is contrary to all experience to say that because a fact is related with incorrect additions and embellishments, therefore it probably never happened at all; or that it is not, in general, easy for an impartial mind to distinguish between the fact and the embellishments. I cannot doubt that the Lyons persecution took place, and that the punishment of Christians for being Christians was sanctioned by Marcus Aurelius. But then I must add that nine modern readers out of ten, when they read this, will, I believe, have a perfectly false notion of what the moral action of Marcus Aurelius, in sanctioning that punishment, really was. They imagine Trajan, or Antoninus Pius, or Marcus Aurelius, fresh from the perusal of the Gospel, fully aware of the spirit and holiness of the Christian saints, ordering their extermination because they loved darkness rather than light. Far from this, the Christianity which these emperors aimed at repressing was, in their conception of it, something philosophically contemptible, politically subversive, and morally abominable. As men, they sincerely regarded it much as well-conditioned people, with us, regard Mormonism; as rulers, they regarded it much as Liberal statesmen, with us, regard the Jesuits. A kind of Mormonism, constituted as a vast secret society, with obscure aims of political and social subversion, was what Antoninus Pius and Marcus Aurelius believed themselves to be repressing when they punished Christians. The early Christian apologists again and again declared to us under what odious imputations the Christians lay, how general was the belief that these disputations were well grounded, how sincere was the horror which the belief inspired. The multitude, convinced that the Christians were atheists who ate human flesh and thought incest no crime, displayed against them a fury so passionate as to embarrass and alarm their rulers. The severe expressions of Tacitus show how deeply the prejudices of the multitude was imbued the educated class also. One asks oneself with astonishment how a doctrine so benign as that of Christ can have incurred misrepresentations so monstrous. The inner and moving cause of the misrepresentation lay, no doubt, in this - that Christianity was a new spirit in the Roman world, destined to act in that world as its dissolvent; and it was inevitable that Christianity in the Roman world, like democracy in the modern world, like every new spirit with a similar mission assigned to it, should at its first appearance occasion an instinctive shrinking and repugnance in the world which it was to dissolve. The outer and palpable causes of the misrepresentation were, for the Roman public at large, the confounding of the Christians with the Jews, that isolated, fierce, and stubborn race, whose stubbornness, fierceness, and isolation, real as they were, the fancy of a civilised Roman yet further exaggerated; the atmosphere of mystery and novelty which surrounded the Christian rites; the very simplicity of Christian theism: for the Roman statesman the character of secret assemblages which the meetings of the Christian community wore, under a State-system as jealous of unauthorised associations as the Code Napoleon.

A Roman of Marcus Aurelius's time and position could not well see the Christians except through the mist of these prejudices. Seen through such a mist, the Christians appeared with a thousand faults not their own; but it has not been sufficiently remarked that faults, really their own, many of them assuredly appeared with besides, faults especially likely to strike such an observer as Marcus Aurelius, and to confirm him in the prejudices of his race, station, and rearing. We look back upon Christianity after it has proved what a future it bore within it, and for us the sole representatives of its early struggles are the pure and devoted spirits through whom it proved this; Marcus Aurelius saw it with its future yet unshown, and with the tares among its professed progeny not less conspicuous than the whet. Who can doubt that among the professing Christians of the nineteenth, there was plenty of folly, plenty of rabid nonsense, plenty of gross fanaticism; who will even venture to affirm that, separated in great measure from the intellect and civilisation of the world for one or two centuries, Christianity, wonderful as have been its fruits, had the development perfectly worthy of its inestimable germ? Who will venture to affirm that, by the alliance of Christianity with the virtue and intelligence of men like the Antonines, of the best product of Greek and Roman civilisation, while Greek and Roman civilisation had yet life and power, Christianity and the world, as well as the Antonines themselves, would not have been gainers? That alliance was not to be; the Antonines lived and died with an utter misconception of Christianity; Christianity grew up in the Catacombs, not on the Palatine. Marcus Aurelius incurs no moral reproach by having authorised the punishment of the Christians; he does not thereby become in the least what we mean by a *persecutor*. One may concede that it was impossible for him to see Christianity as it really was; - as impossible as for even the moderate and sensible Fleury to see the Antonines as they really were; - one may concede that the point of view from which Christianity appeared something anti-civil and anti-social, which the State had the faculty to judge, and the duty to suppress, was inevitably his. Still, however, it remains true, that this sage, who made perfection his aim and reason his law, did Christianity an immense injustice, and rested in an idea of State-attributes which was illusive. And this is, in truth, characteristic of Marcus Aurelius, that he is blameless, yet, in a certain sense, unfortunate; in his character, beautiful as it is, there is something melancholy, circumscribed, and ineffectual.

For of his having such a son as Commodus, too, one must say that he is not to be blamed on that account, but that he is unfortunate. Disposition and temperament are inexplicable things; there are natures on which the best education and example are thrown away; excellent fathers may have, without any fault of theirs, incurably vicious sons. It is to be remembered, also, that Commodus was left at the perilous age of nineteen, master of the world; while his father, at that age, was but beginning a twenty years' apprenticeship to wisdom, labour, and self-command, under the sheltering teachership of his uncle Antoninus. Commodus was a prince apt to be led by favourites; and if the story is true which says that he left, all through his reign, the Christians untroubled, and ascribes this lenity to the influence of his mistress Mercia, it shows that he could be led to good as well as to evil; for

such a nature to be left at a critical age with absolute power, and
wholly without good counsel and direction, was the more fatal. Still
one cannot help wishing that the example of Marcus Aurelius could
have availed more with his own only son; one cannot but think that
with such virtue as his there should go, too, the ardour which removes
mountains might have even won Commodus; the word *ineffectual* again
rises to one's mind; Marcus Aurelius saved his own soul by his
righteousness, and he could do no more. Happy they, who can do this!
But still happier, who can do more!

Yet, when one passes from his outward to his inward life, when
one turns over the pages of his *Meditations* – entries jotted down from
day to day, amid the business of the city or the fatigues of the camp, for
his own guidance and support, meant for no eye but his own, without
the slightest attempt at style, with no care, even, for correct writing,
not to be surpassed for naturalness and sincerity – all disposition to
carp and cavil dies away, and one is overpowered by the charm of a
character of such purity, delicacy, and virtue. He fails neither in small
things nor in great; he keeps watch over himself both that the great
springs of action may be right in him, and that the minute details of
action may be right also, how admirable in a hard-tasked ruler, and a
ruler, too, with a passion for thinking and reading is such a
memorandum as the following:

'Not frequently nor without necessity to say to any one, or to
write in a letter, that I have no leisure; nor continually to excuse the
neglect of duties required by our relation to those with whom we live,
by alleging urgent occupation'.

And when that ruler is a Roman emperor, what an 'idea' is this to
be written down and meditated by him:

'The idea of a polity in which there is the same law for all, a
polity administered with regard to equal rights and equal
freedom of speech, and the idea of a kingly government which

respects most of all the freedom of the governed.'
And, for all men who 'drive at practice', what practical rules may
not one accumulate out of these *Meditations*:

'The greatest part of what we say or do being unnecessary, if a
man takes this away, he will have more leisure and less
uneasiness. Accordingly, on every occasion a man should ask
himself, is this one of the unnecessary things? Now a man
should take away not only unnecessary acts, but also unnecessary
thoughts, for thus superfluous acts will not follow after.'

And again:

'We ought to check in the series of our thoughts everything that
is without a purpose and useless, but most of all the over-
curious feeling and the malignant; and a man should use himself
to think of those things only about which if one should
suddenly ask "What hast thou now in thy thoughts?" with
perfect openness thou mightest immediately answer "This or
That"; so that from thy words it should be plain that everything
in thee is simple and benevolent, and such as befits a social
animal, and one that cares not for thoughts about sensual
enjoyments, or any rivalry or envy and suspicion, or anything
else for which thou wouldst blush if thou shouldst say thou
hadst it in thy mind.'

So, with a stringent practicalness worthy of Benjamin Franklin,
he discourses on his favourite text, *Let nothing be done without a
purpose*. But it is when he enters the region where Franklin
cannot follow him, when he utters his thoughts on the ground-
motives of human action, that he is most interesting – that he
becomes the unique, the incomparable Marcus Aurelius.

Christianity uses language very liable to be misunderstood when it seems to tell men to do good, not, certainly, from the vulgar motives of self-interest, or vanity, or love of human praise, but that 'their Father which seeth in secret may reward them openly'. The motives of reward and punishment have come, from the misconception of language of this kind, to be strangely over-pressed by many Christian moralists, to the deterioration and disfigurement of Christianity. Marcus Aurelius says, truly and nobly:

'One man, when he has done a service to another, is ready to set it down to his account as a favour conferred. Another is not ready to do this, but still in his own mind he thinks of the man as his debtor, and he knows what he ahs done. A third in a manner does not even know what he has done, *but he is like a vine which has produced grapes, and seeks for nothing more after it has once produced its proper fruit.* As a horse when he has run, a dog when he has caught the game, a bee when it has made its honey, so a man, when he has done a good act, does not call out for others to come and see, but he goes on to another act, as a vine goes on to produce again the grapes in season. Must a man, then, be one of these, who in a manner acts thus without observing it? Yes'.

And again:

'What more dost thou want when thou hast done a man a service? Art thou not content that thou hast done something conformable to thy nature, and dost thou seek to be paid for it, *just as if the eye demanded a recompense for seeing or the feet for walking?'*

Christianity, in order to match morality of this strain, has to correct its apparent offers of external reward, and to say: *The kingdom of God is within you.*

I have said that it is by its accent of emotion that the morality of Marcus Aurelius acquires a special character, and reminds on of Christian morality. The sentences of Seneca are stimulating to the intellect; the sentences of Epictetus are fortifying to the character; the sentences of Marcus Aurelius find their way to the soul. I have said that religious emotion has the power to *light up* morality; the emotion of Marcus Aurelius does not quite light up his morality, but it suffuses it; it has not power to melt the clouds of effort and austerity quite away, but it shines through them and glorifies them; it is a spirit, not so much of gladness and elation, as of gentleness and sweetness; a delicate and tender sentiment, which is less than joy and more than resignation. He says that in his youth he learned from Maximus, one of his teachers, 'cheerfulness in all circumstances as well as in illness; *and a just admixture in the moral character of sweetness and dignity"*; and it is this very admixture of sweetness with his dignity which makes him so beautiful a moralist. It enables him to carry even into his observation of nature, a delicate penetration, a sympathetic tenderness, worthy of Wordsworth; the spirit of such a remark as the following seems to me to have no parallel in the whole range of Greek and Roman literature:

'Figs, when they are quite ripe, gape open; and in the ripe olives the very circumstance of their being near to rottenness adds a peculiar beauty to the fruit. And the ears of corn bending down, and the lion's eyebrows, and the foam which flows from the mouth of wild boars, and many other things, though they are far from being beautiful, in a certain sense, still, because they come in the course of nature, have a beauty in them, and they please the mind; so that if a man should have a feeling and a deeper insight with respect to the things which are produced in the universe, there is hardly anything which comes in the course of nature which will not seem to him to be in a manner disposed so as to give pleasure.'

But it is when his strain passes to directly moral subjects that his delicacy and sweetness lend to it the greatest charm. Let those who can feel the beauty of spiritual refinement read this, the reflection of an emperor who prized mental superiority highly:

'Thou sayest "Men cannot admire the sharpness of thy wits". Be it so; but there are many other things of which thou canst not say "I am not formed for them by nature". Show those qualities, then, which are altogether in thy power — sincerity, gravity, endurance of labour, aversion to pleasure, contentment with thy portion and with few things, benevolence, frankness, no love of superfluity, freedom from trifling, magnanimity. Dost thou not see how many qualities thou art at once able to exhibit, as to which there is no excuse of natural incapacity and unfitness, and yet thou still remainest voluntarily below the mark? Or art thou compelled, through being defectively furnished by nature, to murmur, and to be mean, and to flatter, and to find fault with thy poor body, and to try to please men, and to make great display, and to be so restless in thy mind? No, indeed; but thou mightest have been delivered from these things long ago. Only, if in truth thou canst be charged with being rather slow and dull of comprehension, thou must exert thyself about this also, not neglecting nor yet taking pleasure in thy dullness.'

The same sweetness enables him to fix his mind, when he sees the isolation and moral death caused by sin, not on the cheerless thought of the misery of this condition, but on the inspiriting thought that man is blest with the power to escape from it:

'Suppose that thou hast detached thyself from the natural unity – for thou wast made by nature a part, but now thou has cut thyself off – yet here is this beautiful provision, that it is in thy power again to unite thyself. God has allowed this to no other part after it has been separated and cut asunder, to come together again. But consider the goodness with which he has privileged man; for he has put it in his power, when he has been separated, to return and to be united, and to assume his place.'

It enables him to control even the passion for retreat and solitude, so strong in a soul like his, to which the world could offer no abiding city:

'Men seek retreat for themselves, houses in the country, sea-shores, and mountains' and thou, too, art wont to desire such things very much. But this is altogether a mark of the most common sort of men, for it is in thy power whenever thou shalt choose to retire into thyself. For nowhere either with more quiet or more freedom from trouble does a man retire than into his own soul, particularly when he has within him such thoughts that by looking into them he is immediately in perfect tranquility. Constantly, then, give to thyself this retreat, and renew thyself; and let thy principles be brief and fundamental, which, as soon as thou shalt recur to them, will be sufficient to cleanse the soul completely, and to send thee back free from all discontent with the things to which thou returnest.'

Against this feeling of discontent and weariness, so natural to the great for whom there seems nothing left to desire or to strive after, but so enfeebling to them, so deteriorating, Marcus Aurelius never ceased to struggle. With resolute thankfulness he kept in remembrance the blessings of his lot, the true blessings of it, not the false:

'I have to thank Heaven that I was subjected to a ruler and father (Antoninus Pius) who was able to take away all pride from me, and to bring me to the knowledge that it is possible for a man to live in a palace without either guards or embroidered dresses, or any show of this kind; but that it is in such a man's power to bring himself very near to the fashion of a private person, without being for this reason either meaner in thought or more remiss in action with respect to the things which must be done for public interest ... I have to be thankful that my children have not been stupid nor deformed in body; that I did not make more proficiency in rhetoric, poetry, and the other studies, by which I should perhaps have been completely engrossed, if I had seen that I was making great progress in them; ... that I know Apollonius, Rusticus, Maximus; ... that I received clear and frequent impressions about living according to nature, and what kind of a life that is, so that, so far as depended on Heaven, and its gifts, help, and inspiration, nothing hindered me from forthwith living according to nature, though I still fall short of it through my own fault, and through not observing the admonitions of Heaven, and, I may almost say, its direct instructions; that my body has held out so long in such a kind of life as mine; that though it was my mother's lot to die young, she spent the last years of her life with me; that whenever I wished to help any man in his need, I was never told that I had not the means of doing it; that, when I had an inclination to philosophy, I did not fall into the hands of a sophist.'

And, as he dwelt with gratitude on these helps and blessings vouchsafed to him, his mind (so, at least, it seems to me) would sometimes revert with awe to the perils and temptations of the lonely height where he stood, to the lives of Tiberius, Caligula, Nero, Domitian, in their hideous blackness and ruin; and then he wrote down for himself such a warning entry as this, significant and terrible in its abruptness:

'A black character, a womanish character, a stubborn character, bestial, childish, animal, stupid, counterfeit, scurrilous, fraudulent, tyrannical!'

or this:

'About what am I now employing my soul? On every occasion I must ask myself this question, and inquire. What have I now in this part of me which they call the ruling principal, and whose soul have I now? – that of a child, or of a young man, or of a weak woman, or of a tyrant, or of one of the lower animals in the service of man, or of a wild beast?'

The character he wished to attain he knew well, and beautifully he has marked it, and marked, too, his sense of shortcoming:

'When thou hast assumed these names – good, modest, true, rational, equal-minded, magnanimous – take care that thou dost not change these names; and, if thou shouldst lose them, quickly return to them. If thou maintainest thyself in possession of these names without desiring that others should call thee by them, thou wilt be another being, and wilt enter on another life. For to continue to be such as thou hast hitehrto been, and to be torn in pieces and defiled in such a life, is the character of a very stupid man, and one overfond of his life and like those half-devoured fighters with wild beasts, who though covered with wounds and gore still entreat to be kept to the following day, though they will be exposed in the same state to the same claws and bits. Therefore fix thyself in the possession of these few names: and if thou art able to abide in them, abide as if thou was removed to the Happy Islands.'

For all his sweetness and serenity, however, man's point of life 'between two infinities' (of that expression Marcus Aurelius is the real owner) was to him anything but a Happy Island, and the performances on it he saw through no veils of illusion. Nothing is in general more gloomy and monotonous than declamations on the hollowness and transitoriness of human life and grandeur: but here, too, the great charm of Marcus Aurelius, his emotion, comes in to relieve the monotony and to break through the gloom; and even on this eternally used topic, he is imaginative, fresh, and striking:

'Consider, for example, the times of Vespasian. Thou wilt see all these things, people marrying, bringing up children, sick, dying, warring, feasting, trafficking, cultivating the ground, flattering, obstinately arrogant, suspecting, plotting, wishing for somebody to die, grumbling about the present, loving, heaping up treasure, desiring to be consuls or kings. Well then, that life of these people no longer exists at all. Again, go to the times of Trajan. All again the same. Their life too is gone. But chiefly thou shouldst think of those whom thou hast thyself known distracting themselves about idle things, neglecting to do what was in accordance with their proper constitution, and to hold firmly to this and to be content with it.'

Again:

'The things which are much valued in life are empty, and rotten, and trifling; and people are like little dogs biting one another, and little children quarrelling, crying, and then straight-way laughing. But fidelity, and modesty, and justice, and truth, are fled
Up to Olympus from the wide-spread earth.
What then is there which still detains thee here?'

And once more:

'Look down from above on the countless herds of men, and their countless solemnities, and the infinitely varied voyaging in storms and calms, and differences among those who are born, who live together, and die. And consider too the life lived by others in olden time, and the life now lived among barbarous nations, and how many know not even thy name, and how many will soon forget it, and how they who perhaps now are praising thee will very soon blame thee, and that neither a posthumous name is of any value, nor reputation, nor anything else.'

He recognised, indeed, that (to use his own words) 'the prime principle in man's constitution is the social', and he laboured sincerely to make not only his acts towards his fellow-men, but his thoughts also, suitable to this conviction:

'When thou wishest to delight thyself, think of the virtues of those who live with thee, for instance, the activity of one, and the modesty of another, and the liberality of a third, and some other good quality of a fourth.'

Still, it is hard for a pure and thoughtful man to live in a state of rapture at the spectacle afforded to him by his fellow-creatures; above all is it hard, when such a man is placed as Marcus Aurelius was placed, and has had the meanness and perversity of his fellow-creatures thrust in no common measure upon his notice – has had, time after time, to experience how 'within ten days thou wilt seem a god to those to whom thou art now a beast and an ape'. His true strain of thought as to his relations with his fellow-men is rather the following. He had been enumerating the higher consolations which may support a man at the approach of death, and he goes on:

'But if thou requirest also a vulgar kind of comfort which shall reach thy heart, thou wilt be made best reconciled to death by observing the objects from which thou art going to be removed, and the morals of those with whom thy soul will no longer be mingled. For it is no way right to be offended with men, but it is thy duty to care for them and to bear with them gently; and yet to remember that thy departure will not be from men who have the same principles as thyself. For this is the only thing, if there be any, which could draw us the contrary way and attach us to life, to be permitted to live with those who have the same principles as ourselves. But now thou seest how great is the distress caused by the difference of those who live together, so that thou mayst say: "Come quick, O death, lest perchance I too should forget myself." '

O faithless and perverse generation! How long shall I be with you? How long shall I suffer you? Sometimes this strain rises even to passion:[9]

'Short is the little which remains to thee of life. Live as on a mountain. Let men see, let them know, a real man, who lives as he was meant to live. If they cannot endure him, let them kill him. For that is better than to live as men do.'

It is remarkable how little of a merely local and temporary character, how little of those *scoriæ* which a reader has to clear away before he gets to the precious ore, how little that even admits of doubt or question, the morality of Marcus Aurelius exhibits. In general, the action he prescribes is action which every sound nature must recognise as right, and the motives he assigns are motives which every clear reason must recognise as valid. And so he remains the especial friend and comforter of all scrupulous and difficult, yet pure and upward-striving souls, in those ages most especially that walk by sight not by faith, that have no open vision; he cannot give such souls, perhaps, all they yearn for, but he gives them much; and what he gives them, they can receive. Yet no, it is not on this account that such souls love him most, it is rather because of the emotion which gives to his

---

[9] Perhaps there is one exception. He is fond of urging as a motive for man's cheerful acquiescence in whatever befalls him, that 'whatever happens to every man *is for the interest of the universal*'! that the whole contains nothing *which is not for its advantage*; that everything which happens to a man is to be accepted, 'even if it seems disagreeable, *because it leads to the health of the universe*'. And the whole course of the universe, he adds, has a providential reference to man's welfare 'all other things have been made for the sake of rational beings'. Religion has in all ages freely used this language, and it is not religion which will object to Marcus Aurelius's use of it; but Science can hardly accept as severely accurate this employment of the terms *interest* and *advantage*; even to a sound nature and a clear reason the proposition that things happen 'for the interest of the universal', as men conceive of interest, may seem to have no meaning at all, and the proposition that 'all things have been made for the sake of rational beings' may seem to be false. Yet even to this language, not irresistibly cogent when it is thus absolutely used, Marcus Aurelius gives a turn which makes it true and useful, when he says 'The ruling part of man can make a material for itself out of that which opposes it, as fire lays hold of what falls into it, and rises higher by means of this very material'. When he says 'What else are all things except exercises for the reason? Persevere then until thou shalt have made all things thine own, as the stomach which is strengthened makes all things its own, as the blazing fire makes flame and brightness out of everything that is thrown into it'. When he says 'Thou wilt not cease to be miserable till thy mind is in such a condition, that, what luxury is to those who enjoy pleasure, such shall be to thee, in every matter which presents itself, the doing of the things which are conformable to man's constitution; for a man ought to consider as an enjoyment everything which it is in his power to do according to his own Nature and it is in his power everywhere'. In this sense it is most true that 'all things have been made for the sake of rational beings'; that 'all things work together for good'.

voice so touching an accent, it is because he, too yearns as they do for something unattained by him. What an affinity for Christianity had this persecutor of the Christians! The effusion of Christianity, its relieving tears, its happy self-sacrifice, were the very element, one feels, for which his spirit longed: they were near him, he touched them, he passed them by. One feels, too, that the Marcus Aurelius one knows must still have remained, even had they presented themselves to him, in a great measure himself; he would have been no Justin: but how would they have affected him? In what measure would they have changed him? Granted that he might have found, like the Alogi in ancient and modern times, in the most beautiful of the Gospels, the Gospel which has leavened Christendom most powerfully, the Gospel of St John, too much Greek metaphysics, too much *gnosis*; granted that this Gospel might have looked too like what he knew already to be a total surprise to him: what, then, would he have said to the Sermon on the Mount? To the twenty-sixth chapter of St Matthew? What would have become of his notions of the *exitiabilis superstitio*, of the 'obstinacy of the Christians'? Vain question! Yet the greatest charm of Marcus Aurelius is that he makes us ask it. We see him wise, just, self governed tender, thankful, blameless; yet, with all this, agitated, stretching out his arms for something beyond.

STOICISM

APPENDIX II.

Stoicism was so called from the Colonnade at Athens, where Zeno, about 300 bc, first taught its doctrines. More religious in character than any other Greek philosophy, it brought a new moral force into the world. It put intellectual speculation more into the background, and carried the moral attitude of the Cynics further into the domain of right conduct. Oriental fervor was in it grafted on Greek acumen, for Zeno was a Phoenician Greek of Cyprus, and Chrysippus, the St Paul who defined and established Stoicism, a Cilician like the Apostle.

In spite of its origin Stoicism proved wonderfully adapted to the practical Roman character, and under the tyranny of the early Caesars it formed the only impregnable fortress of liberty for the noblest Romans. It reached its culmination, and found its highest exponents as a living creed in the courtier Seneca, the Phrygian slave Epictetus, and the emperor Marcus Antoninus.

Stoic philosophy consisted of Logic, Physics, and Ethics. Logic, which comprised Dialectics and Rhetoric, was the necessary instrument of all speculation; but Marcus found no satisfaction in either branch of it, nor in such Physics as dealt with Meteorology.

The keynote of Stoicism was *Life according to nature*, and Marcus was converted to the pursuit of this possibly by Sextus the Boeotian. By "Nature" was meant the controlling Reason of the Universe. A study of physics was necessary for a proper understanding of the cosmos and our position in it, and thus formed the scientific basis of philosophy; but it was regarded as strictly subordinate, and merely a means to an end.

Though he confesses to some disappointment in his progress therein, there is no doubt that Marcus was well versed in Stoic Physics. Fully recognizing the value of a scientific spirit of inquiry, he describes it as a characteristic of the rational soul to "go the whole Universe through and grasp its plan," affirming that "no man can be good without correct notions as to the Nature of the Whole and his own constitution."

To the Stoics, the Universe – God and matter – was one, all substance, unified by the close "sympathy" and interdependence of the parts, forming with the rational Power, that was co-extensive with it, a single entity. The Primary Being, by means of its informing Force, acting as igneous or atmospheric current upon inert matter, evolved out of itself a Cosmos, subsequent modifications being by way of consequence. This Universe is periodically destroyed by fire, thus returning again to its pristine Being, only, however, to be created anew on the same plan even to the smallest details; and so on for ever.

God and matter being thus indistinguishable, for all that was not God in its original form was God in an indirect sense as a manifestation of him, the Stoic creed was inevitably pantheistic. It was also materialistic; for the Stoics, allowing existence to nothing incorporeal, by means of their strange theory of air-currents inherent even in abstract things such as virtue, rendered not only them but God himself corporeal, terming him the "perfect living Being." But their conceptions on this point seem to be really irreconcilable, for while on the one hand they speak of the Supreme power by such names as

Zeus, Cause or Force, Soul, Mind, or Reason of the Universe, Law or Truth, Destiny, Necessity, Providence, or Nature of the Whole, on the other they identify it with such terms as Fiery Fluid, or Heat, Ether (warm air), or Pneuma (atmospheric current).

Other physical theories were borrowed from Heraclitus, and Marcus constantly alludes to these, such as the "downward and upward" round of the elements as they emanate from the primary Fire, air passing into fire, fire into earth, earth into water and so back again, and the famous doctrine that all things are in flux.

Man consists of Body, Soul, Intelligence, or Flesh, Pneuma, and the Ruling Reason. But the Soul can be looked upon in two ways as an exhalation from blood, and as the Ruling Reason. It is the latter, a "morsel" or "efflux" from the Divine, which constitutes the real man. Marcus often speaks of this rational nature of a man as his daemon, or genius enthroned within him, and makes the whole problem of life depend upon how this Reason treats itself. As all that is rational is akin, we are formed for fellowship with others and, the Universe being one, what affects a part of it affects the whole. Reason is as a Law to all rational creatures, and so we are all citizens of a World-state. In this cosmopolitanism the Stoics approached the Christian view, ethics being divorced from national politics and made of universal application. It was no cloistered virtue the Stoics preached, showing how a man can save his own soul, but a practical positive goodness; though it cannot be denied that the claims of the self-sufficiency of the Inner Self and social interdependence of parts of a common whole are not easy to reconcile. It is certain, however, that the Stoic admission of slaves into the brotherhood of man had an ameliorating effect upon slavery, and the well known bias of Marcus in favor of enfranchisement may well have been due to his creed.

From virtue alone can happiness and peace of mind result, and virtue consists in submission to the Higher Power and all that he sends us, in mastery over our animal nature, in freedom from all perturbation, and in the entire independence of the Inner Self. Since life is opinion and everything but what we think it, the vital question is what assent we give to the impressions of our senses. "Wipe out imagination," says Marcus, time after time, "and you are saved." "Do not think of yourself hurt and you remain unhurt." He longs for the day when he shall cease to be duped by his impressions and pulled like a puppet by his passions, and his soul shall be in a great calm. But virtue must also show itself, like faith, in right actions. It means not only self-control but justice and benevolence to others and piety toward the Gods.

By the Gods Marcus sometimes means the controlling Reason, sometimes, apparently, Gods in a more popular sense, such as are even visible to the eyes. He often puts the alternative God (or Gods) and Atoms, but himself firmly believes that there are immortal Gods who care for mankind, live with them, and help even bad men. He bids himself call upon them, follow them, be their minister, live with them, and be likened to them. They too are part of the Cosmos and subject to its limitations, and by our own loyalty to Destiny we contribute to the welfare and permanence of God himself. But a predestined Order of things involved fatalism, and the Stoics were hard put to it to maintain the complete freedom of the will.

Unfortunately the Stoic scheme left no room for Immortality. At most a soul could only exist till the next conflagration, when it must be absorbed again into the Primary Being. Seneca indeed, who was no true Stoic, speaks in almost Christian terms of a new and blissful life to come, but Epictetus turns resolutely, and Marcus with evident reluctance, from a hope so dear to the human heart. In one place the latter even uses the expression "another life," and finds it a hard saying that the souls of those who were in closest communion with God should die forever when they die. But he does not repine. He is ready for either fate, extinction, or transference elsewhere.

One more question remains, that of suicide. The Stoics allowed this, if circumstances made it impossible for a man to maintain his moral standard. The door is open, but the call must be very clear. Still the act seems quite inconsistent with the doctrine of submission to Destiny, and the classing of things external as indifferent.

In this brief sketch of Stoicism much has perforce been omitted, and much may seem obscure, but Marcus confesses that "things are in a manner so wrapped up in mystery that even the Stoics have found them difficult to apprehend." This at least we know, that Stoicism inspired some of the noblest lives ever lived, left its humanizing impress upon the Roman law, which we have inherited, and appeals in an especial way to some of the higher instincts of our nature.

APPENDIX III. BIBLIOGRAPHY

1   The premier edition from the lost palatine MS., issued in 1558, with a Latin translation by Xylander (i.e. W. Hozmann of Augsberg).

2   Meric Casaubon's first edition of the original Greek in 1643. Reprinted 1680.

3   Thomas Gataker's edition, published in 1652 at Cambridge with a new Latin version and voluminous notes including contributions from Saumaise (Salm), Boot, and Junius. Reprinted 1696, 1704, 1707, 1729 (Wolle and Buddeus), 1744, 1751, 1775 (Morus).

4   Jo. Matth. Schultz, editions 1802 (Sleswig), 1820 (Leipzig), 1842 (Paris). Menagius and Reiske supplied notes to Schultz.

5   A. Coraes, in vol. Iv: Paris, 1816. This editor has made more successful emendations of the text than any other.

6   Nicholas Bach, *De Marco Aurelio Antonino*, Lipsiae, 1826.

7   Alexis Pierron, *Pensées de l'Empéreur Marc Aurèle Antonin*, Paris, 1843 (with introduction and notes).

8   Edition by C. L. Porcher, New York, 1863. Proof sheets of this, with additional notes are in the British Museum.

9   Panag. Schaphidiotes, [title?] Athens, 1881.
    Jo. Stich, "Adnotationes criticae ad M. Antoninum,"
    Programm der K. Studienanstatt, Zweibrücken,
    1880/1. The same editor brought out an edition for
    the Teubner Series in 1882, and a second revised
    edition in 1903, with valuable introductions and
    index.

August Nauck, "De M. Antonini Commentariis," 1882,
    *Bulletin de l'Académie impériale des Sciences de St
    Petersbourg* (28), pp. 196-210. See also "Mélanges
    Gréco-Romains" ii, pp. 743-5.

12 Hermann J. Polak, "In Marci Antonini Commentarios
    analecta critica," *Hermes* xxi, (1886), pp. 321-356,
    and *Sylloge commentationum guam C. Conto obtulerunt
    philologi Batavi,* Lugd. Bat., 1894, pp. 85-94.

13 G. H. Rendall, "On the text of M. Aurelius
    Antoninus," *Journal of Philology,* xxiii, pp. 116-160.

14 Ulrich de Wilamowitz-Moellendorf, *Griechisces
    Lesebuch ii,* Berlin 1902, pp. 311-320.

15 P. Hoffmann, "Notes critiques sur Marc Aurèle," *Revue
    de l'Instruction publique en Belgique,* xlvii, 1904,
    pp. 11-23.

16 Adolf Sonny, "Zur Ueberlieferung Geschichte von
    M.A.," *Philologus* 54, pp. 181-3.

17 J. H. Leopold, "Ad M. Antonini commentarios," *Mnemosyne* xxxi, 1902, pp. 341–364; xxxiv, 1907, pp. 63–82. He also brought out a new edition of the Greek text for the Clarendon press in 1911.

18 Paul Fournier, "Pensées de Marc Aurèle." Traduction d'Auguste Couat éditée par p. Fournier. Paris, 1904. There are numerous notes.

19 Herbert Richards, "Notes on Marcus Aurelius," *Classical Quarterly,* xix, Feb. 1905, pp. 18–21.

20 A. J. Kronenberg, "Ad M. Antoninum," *Classical Review,* xix, July, 1905, pp. 301–3.

21 Karl Fr. W. Schmidt, " Textkritische Bemerkungen zu Mark Aurel," *Hermes,* xii, 1907, pp. 595–607.

22 A. P. Lemercier, "Les Pensées de Marc Aurèle," Paris, 1910, with notes and a good introduction.

23 Heinrich Schenkl, a new edition of the *Thoughts* for the Teubner Press, 1913. The latest and most complete edition with valuable introductions and full indices. The same editor has also published "Zurhandscriftlichen Ueberlieferung von Marcus Antoninus" (*Eranos Vindobonensis,* 1893) and "Zum erste Buche des Selbstbetrachtungen des Kaisers Marcus Antoninus" (Wiener Studien, 1912).

24 C. R. Haines, *Marcus Aurelius*, Harvard University Press, Loeb Classical Series, 1916.

25 C. R. Haines, "The Composition and Chronology of the *Thoughts* of Marcus Aurelius," *Journal of Philology*, vol. xxxiii, No. 66, pp.278-295.

For the history and doctrines of Stoicism, besides the standard work of Zeller and the treatise on *Roman Stoicism* by E. V. Arnold, the following will be found useful: N Bach (mentioned above), 1826; H. Doergens, "de comparatione Antoninianae philosophiae cum L. Annaei Senecae," 1816; the admirable essay on Stoicism by G. H. Rendall, prefixed to his edition of 1898; *Greek and Roman Stoicism* by C. H. S. Davis, 1903; and *Stoic and Christian* by Leonard Alston, 1906.

We also have:

A. L. Trannoy, *Pensées*, edited with French translation, Budé, Paris, 1925.

F. Martinazzoli, *La Successio d. Marco Aurelio. Struttura e spirito del primo l. dei Pensieri*, Bari, 1951.

H. R. Neuenschwander, *Mark Aurels. Beziehungen zu Seneca u. Poseidonius*, Bern, 1951.

A. S. L. Farquharson, *Meditations*, edited with English translation. I. Oxford, 1944.

APPNDIX III. BIBLIOGRAPHY

M. Staniforth, Translation in Penguin Books, Harmondsworth (1964), 1966.

A. Birley, *Marcus Aurelius,* London, 1966. Deals with his principate.

M. Forstater, *The Spiritual Teachings of Marcus Aurelius*, Coronet Books, 2000.

J. Scott, *Marcus Aurelius in a Box of Illuminations*, Profile Books, 2001.

G. Hays, Marcus Aurelius' Meditations, Weidenfeld & Nicholson, 2003.

In 1964 Samuel Bronson produced a Hollywood epic, *The Fall of the Roman Empire*. Although historically inexact, the last years of Marcus Aurelius were eloquently acted by Sir Alec Guinness, with a strong supporting cast. The film captured the atmosphere of Ancient Rome.

Also by Alan Jacobs

THE BHAGAVAD GITA

ISBN: 1 903816 51 3   Price: £12.99

The Bhagavad Gita is one of the world's greatest scriptures, the key sacred text of Hinduism. It means the 'Song of God' and is often called the 'Song Celestial'. Alan Jacobs has succeeded in revitalising the ancient text intoa form which reveals the full majesty of this magnificent scripture as well as its practical message for today's seekers.

'Alan Jacobs' poetic rendering of the Gita is intact and profound.
The reader is inspired to enter anew this universal text of wisdom.'

Mira Pagal-Decoux

'I am most impressed. The wonderful philosophy of the famed
Bhagavad Gita has been rendered into modern verse with such
facility and a lovely combination of veracity and freedom. This is
indeed a unique interpretation of the Indian classic.'

Ramesh Balsekar, Advaita Teacher.

'I am absolutely sure that Alan Jacobs has a unique and
indispensable message for the world.'   Douglas Harding

UK orders: 01962 736880
US orders: 1 800 462 6420

THE PRINCIPAL UPANISHADS

ISBN: 1 903816 50 5   Price: £12.99

The origins of the Upanishads, sacred writings of Hinduism, predate recorded history. They are thought of by many as perhaps the greatest of all the books in the history of world religions since they were revealed to the Rishis of the Vedic civilisations some 5,000 to 10,000 years ago. Alan Jacobs has used free modern verse to convey the essential meaning and poetry of the original text, omitting Sanskrit words as much as possible and providing a clear, contemporary commentary.

'I am most impressed, but then, it could not have been otherwise.
There is no better person than Alan Jacobs for this prestigious
job of rendering the ancient Hindu wisdom into free-flowing
modern verse.'

Ramesh Balsekar

'Alan Jacobs recreates these ancient texts of non-dual wisdom in
exquisite poetry. He brings them to life, passing on the essence of
this perennial message in a totally fresh way.'

Mira Pagal-Decoux

UK orders: 01962 736880
US orders: 1 800 462 6420

Also available from O books

The Book of One Dennis Waite

ISBN: 1 903816 41 6   Price: £9.99

Advaita Vedanta quite simply provides the answers to the essential questions of 'life, the universe and all existence.' It is very practical, yet offers explanations satisfying to the intellect. It provides a simple and elegant framework within which all of the problems of life and death may be understood and resolved. The answers are ultimately surprising, and a great relief.

The Book of One is perhaps the most accessible, articulate and relevant book on the nature of non-duality.

'A masterful and profoundly insightful survey of the Advaita teaching and the contemporary scene.'

Alan Jacobs,
Chair, Ramana Maharshi Foundation UK.

———————✳———————

UK orders: 01962 736880
US orders: 1 800 462 6420